# When God Blocks our Path

# When God Blocks Our Path

... And 30 Other Bible-Based Meditations

Roger Ellsworth

*Unless otherwise noted, Scripture quotations are taken from the New King James Version®. Copyright © 1982 by Thomas Nelson. Used by permission. All rights reserved..*

Copyright © 2017, Roger Ellsworth

All rights reserved. No part of this book may be reproduced, scanned, or distributed in any printed or electronic form without permission.

First Edition: 2017

ISBN: 978-0-9988812-4-9

20170707LSI

Great Writing Publications
www.greatwriting.org
Taylors, SC

www.greatwriting.org

# Purpose

*My Coffee Cup Meditations* are short, easy-to-read, engagingly presented devotions based on the Bible, the Word of God. Each reading takes a single idea or theme and develops it in a thought-provoking way so that you are inspired to consider the greatness of God, the relevance of the good news of the life, death, resurrection, and coming-again of Jesus, and are better equipped for life in this world and well prepared for the world to come.

www.mycoffeecupmeditations.com

https://www.facebook.com/MyCoffeeCupMeditations/

# Dedication

Dedicated to the dear saints of Fellowship Baptist Church,
Milan, Tennessee

(Philippians 1:3-6)

# About This Book

This book is the result of the labors Roger Ellsworth and the thought he has given to various passages of Scripture over the years. You may read more about Roger on page 141.

We hope you will enjoy these Bible-based meditations. We would love to hear from you, so please send us a note to tell us what you think—which ones you liked most, and how they made a difference in your life or in the life of a family member, friend, or work associate. To reach us online, go to www.mycoffeecupmeditations.com/contact

# MY COFFEE-CUP MEDITATIONS

# Table of Contents

1 When God Blocks Our Path .................................................. 16
2 Above, Near, Around, and Beneath ..................................... 20
3 Four Men, Two Worlds ......................................................... 24
4 Three Gifts from a Queen ..................................................... 28
5 Which Bird Should I Be? ...................................................... 32
6 The Worst Kind of Forgetfulness ......................................... 36
7 Reminders from Molly .......................................................... 40
8 Mr. Debatable ......................................................................... 44
9 Does the Devil Go to Church? ............................................. 48
10 The Worm Crushing the Mountain ................................... 52
11 Look to the Hippo ................................................................ 56
12 Searching Questions from a Miserable Man ................... 60
13 Should You Growl Like a Bear? ........................................ 64
14 Where to Turn in Times of Trouble ................................... 68
15 A Place and a Peace ............................................................. 72
16 The Words of Jesus .............................................................. 76
17 Quickly Forgotten, Forever Remembered ....................... 80
18 A Message from Ahimaaz ................................................... 84
19 A Hymn Born in Heckling .................................................. 88
20 The Unfailing Friend ........................................................... 92
21 No Continuing City ............................................................. 96
22 David Couldn't Miss, but We Can .................................. 100
23 God's Face Hidden and Unhidden ................................. 104
24 A Rich Dwelling ................................................................. 108
25 What About Christophobia? ............................................ 112

26 Broken Hearts, Numbered Stars .............................................. 116
27 Is Christianity Boring? ................................................................ 120
28 My Favorite Words .................................................................... 124
29 That Great Thing ....................................................................... 128
30 God's Glad Man ........................................................................ 132
31 The Shot That Was Never Fired .............................................. 136

About the Author ........................................................................... 141

# The App

www.mycoffeecupmeditations.com

Be sure you get the app!

# -1-

# From God's Word, the Bible...

*So the churches were strengthened in the faith, and increased in number daily.*
*Now when they had gone through Phrygia and the region of Galatia, they were forbidden by the Holy Spirit to preach the word in Asia. After they had come to Mysia, they tried to go into Bithynia, but the Spirit did not permit them. So passing by Mysia, they came down to Troas. And a vision appeared to Paul in the night. A man of Macedonia stood and pleaded with him, saying, "Come over to Macedonia and help us." Now after he had seen the vision, immediately we sought to go to Macedonia, concluding that the Lord had called us to preach the gospel to them.*

*Acts 16:5-10*

# When God Blocks Our Path

Paul wanted to take the gospel into Asia, but he was "forbidden" by the Holy Spirit. He quickly formed a new plan, namely, to go into Bithynia. But the Spirit of God would not permit this either (v. 7). Some think the means that the Spirit used to thwart Paul's plans was sickness.

Two plans and two disappointments! So Luke, the author of Acts, tells us that Paul and his associates came down to Troas. We may well characterize Troas as the place of disappointment.

Every child of God has spent some time in Troas. We have walked its dark streets, felt the heaviness of its air, and smelled the stench of its stagnant waters.

Why does God put Troas on the itinerary for His children? Why would a loving God allow them to visit such an unpleasant place? Why is it that God seems to block our path?

We might say God has a school there in which He wants

us to enroll. He sends us to Troas so He can teach us important lessons.

We don't know why it was necessary for Paul to visit Troas, but God knew. We do know this—Troas is never an accident. Our disappointments come to us in God's wise design. They wean us away from our self-sufficiency and cause us to cast ourselves in humble dependence on Him. Through our disappointments, God teaches us not to rely on our own understanding but rather to trust wholeheartedly in Him as the One who always has our best interests at heart (Prov. 3:5-6; Rom. 8:28).

When disappointments come our way, we may be inclined to think that God has failed us and forsaken us. But Scripture assures us that such things are never the case. God went with Paul to Troas. He gave Paul a vision in which a man from Macedonia "stood and pleaded" with him, saying: "Come over to Macedonia and help us" (v. 9).

The Lord never sends His people into difficult circumstances without going with them into those circumstances (Isa. 49:16; Matt. 28:20; Heb. 13:5).

If God is with us in our disappointments, the thing we must do to help ourselves face those disappointments is focus on Him. We might say that the best thing to do when facing Troas is to delight ourselves in God instead of questioning Him.

The prophet Habakkuk learned this. He was disappointed that God would use the Babylonians as His instrument to bring judgment on the people of Judah. Habakkuk learned to say:

> *Though the fig tree may not blossom,*
> *Nor fruit be on the vines;*
> *Though the labor of the olive may fail,*
> *And the fields yield no food;*

> *Though the flock be cut off from the fold,*
> *And there be no herd in the stalls—*
> *Yet I will rejoice in the LORD,*
> *I will joy in the God of my salvation.*
> (Hab. 3:17-18)

It is important to note that nothing had changed in Habakkuk's circumstances when he resolved to rejoice in the Lord. The people of Judah were still sinful, and judgment was still coming. Habakkuk rejoiced because in the midst of trying circumstances, he still had God and God's salvation.

The salvation believers enjoy through Christ always puts them in a happy position—so much so that they can say they would rather have salvation with bad circumstances than not to have it with good circumstances. Believers on their worst day are always better off than unbelievers on their best day.

Troas was not a permanent place for Paul. It wasn't long until he and his company were on their way to even greater usefulness for God. God's people never enjoy it when He blocks their path. They would never choose to put it on their itinerary. But as they take the road out, they can be grateful that God put it on their itinerary. As they reflect on it, they may well join Robert Browning Hamilton in saying:

> *I walked a mile with pleasure,*
> *She chattered all the way;*
> *But she left me none the wiser*
> *For all she had to say.*
>
> *I walked a mile with sorrow,*
> *Not one word said she;*
> *But, oh, the things I learned*
> *When sorrow walked with me.*

# -2-

# From God's Word, the Bible...

*There is no one like the God of Jeshurun,*
*Who rides the heavens to help you,*
*And in His excellency on the clouds.*
*The eternal God is your refuge,*
*And underneath are the everlasting arms;*
*He will thrust out the enemy from before you,*
*And will say, "Destroy!"*

*Deuteronomy 33:26-27*

# Above, Near, Around, and Beneath

After leading the people of Israel for forty years, the time has come for Moses to say goodbye. In Deuteronomy 33 we have his farewell address. It falls into three easily discernible parts. There is an introductory statement (vv. 2-5), a blessing for the nation's individual tribes (vv. 6-25) and a closing blessing on the nation (vv. 26-29).

That closing blessing … what wonderful nuggets of truth it contains! How they must have cheered the hearts of the listening Israelites! Here they are: God is above you, near you, around you, and beneath you. Put them all together, and you have Moses saying this to Israel—God is totally sufficient for you.

God above them? Yes, here it is:

> *There is no one like the God of Jeshurun,*
> *Who rides the heavens…*

The name "Jeshurun," meaning "upright one," may have been an affectionate term for the nation of Israel. This much we know for sure—Moses wanted his people to understand that there was no one who could compare to their God. They were poised to enter the land of Canaan. There they would encounter many new gods, but their God was the true God and over all other gods.

God was also near them:

*...Who rides the heavens to help you...*

Does that mean God was near them? Sure, it does. One has to be near to help.

The Israelites had already experienced God's nearness—abundantly so! He drew near or came down (Ex. 2:8) to deliver their fathers from slavery in the land of Egypt. And He would be near to help this new generation as they faced the challenges ahead.

What about the truth that God was around them? Where do we find it? It's right here:

*The eternal God is your refuge...*

When the people of Israel entered the land of Canaan, they would find many refuges, that is, cities with high walls. The Canaanites were surrounded and protected by those walls. The Israelites, on the other hand, dwelled in flimsy tents. How could they, a tent-dwelling people, hope to conquer those mighty fortresses?

Moses assured them that God would be their refuge or fortress. He would surround and protect them as those imposing walls protected the Canaanites.

So we come to the final truth—God was beneath them. Moses says:

*And underneath are the everlasting arms...*

The challenges facing the people of Israel were so daunting that the Israelites would sometimes feel as if they were falling into failure. Moses assured them that God would be there to catch and lift them.

An ancient leader saying farewell to an ancient people! Is that all we have here? No, there is more, and the more is that the truths Moses put before Israel are just as much for us as they were for them.

- God is *above* us. He is the same God now as He was then. He was not limited in wisdom and power in Moses' time, and He is not limited today. He is ever the sovereign ruler of the universe who is greater than all the forces of evil.
- God is *near* us. He is as near to us as He was to Israel of old. God drew near when He sent His Son and told Joseph to call Him "Immanuel," which means "God with us." Our Immanuel is the one who has promised to be with us always (Matt. 28:20).
- God is *around* us. He has surrounded us with the walls of salvation which protect us from eternal loss (Isa. 26:2). That salvation is found in the Lord Jesus Christ who bore on the cross the penalty for sinners so that all who trust in Him in His atoning death will never have to bear that penalty themselves.
- God is *beneath* us. Christians will never be perfect in this life. Oftentimes we fail. And Satan is eager to suggest that failure means that God will have nothing more to do with us. It is not true. No saint of God can ever fall so far that the arms of God are not there to catch and lift him or her.

# -3-

# From God's Word, the Bible...

*So he answered, "Do not fear, for those who are with us are more than those who are with them." And Elisha prayed, and said, "LORD, I pray, open his eyes that he may see." Then the LORD opened the eyes of the young man, and he saw. And behold, the mountain was full of horses and chariots of fire all around Elisha.*

*From 2 Kings 6:8-17*

*(Read 2 Kings 6 for this meditation.)*

# Four Men, Two Worlds

There are four men in this passage of Scripture, and I think I must be here as well. The king of Syria is here. He was one who had no regard for the one and only true God. The king of Israel is also here. He was a man who professed faith in the living God but actually lived in defiance of Him. The prophet Elisha is here. He was a man of towering faith who lived in close communion with the Lord.

I certainly hope I am not either of these two kings. I know I am not the prophet Elisha—not on my very best day. I think I must be the fourth man in this passage—the servant of Elisha. He is the man who cried out to his master: "Alas ... what shall we do?" I wonder if you find yourself in this man? But let's back up a little.

The king of Syria was all aflutter. He was trying to wage war on the king of Israel, but it wasn't going well. Someone was telling Israel's king every move that he, the king of Syria, was about to make. Thinking he had a traitor among his servants, he called them together. It was then that he discovered his problem. One of his servants let the cat out of the bag: "… Elisha, the prophet who is in Israel, tells the king of Israel the words that you speak in your bedroom" (v. 12).

So the king of Syria decided to send a "great army" to Dothan, where Elisha was, to take him into custody.

It was nighttime when the army arrived and surrounded the city. When Elisha's servant arose and peered through the early morning gloom, he saw the army. There were Syrian soldiers everywhere! That's when he said to Elisha: "Alas, my master! What shall we do?" (v. 15).

Elisha was ready with the answer: "Do not fear, for those who are with us are more than those who are with them" (v. 16). Then Elisha asked the Lord to open his servant's eyes, and the servant saw "horses and chariots of fire all around Elisha" (v. 17).

As I look at our world, it sometimes seems as if there is nothing to see but "Syrians." The enemies of God are so numerous, so powerful, and so ferocious that it often seems that there is no hope, and we tremble for the future of the kingdom of God. It is easy to give in to fear of evil and evil times. There are always plenty of Syrians to see! This passage tells us to overcome our fear of the forces of evil by looking beyond them to the invisible forces of heaven.

We sorely need this passage. It reminds us that this world—the visible world—is not all that there is. There is another world. It is the world of God and the angels. It is the spiritual and eternal world. It is far greater than this world that we can see. It is always aware of what is going on in this world and can at any time break in for the glory of God and the good of God's people.

For a long time Nebuchadnezzar could see nothing but his glorious kingdom of Babylon. But God showed him that there was a far greater kingdom than Babylon and a far greater king than himself (Dan. 4:17). His grandson, Belshazzar, also loved the world that he could see, but then a hand appeared from the world that he could not see and wrote a message that caused him to tremble (Dan. 5).

The key to living in this world is to keep looking by faith at the unseen world. It is to endure as Moses did by "seeing Him who is invisible" (Heb. 11:27).

That unseen world will not always be unseen. We will all have to enter it someday, and the only way to enter it safely is through faith in the Lord Jesus Christ. By the way, He, Jesus, is the greatest evidence of the reality of that world. He came from it and steadily revealed the existence of it in His words, His miracles, His death on the cross, and His resurrection.

# -4-

# From God's Word, the Bible...

*So Mordecai went out from the presence of the king in royal apparel of blue and white, with a great crown of gold and a garment of fine linen and purple; and the city of Shushan rejoiced and was glad. The Jews had light and gladness, joy and honor. And in every province and city, wherever the king's command and decree came, the Jews had joy and gladness, a feast and a holiday. Then many of the people of the land became Jews, because fear of the Jews fell upon them.*

*Esther 8:15-17*

# Three Gifts from a Queen

The queen I have in mind is Esther, a beautiful Jewish woman who, through a very unlikely chain of events, rose from obscurity to become queen of Persia at some point in the time span of 485-464 B.C.

The book of Esther tells us of her heroism during a time of crisis. When we read this book, which is one of only two in the Bible that bears the name of a woman, it is as if Esther herself were standing before us and extending her hands to offer three gifts.

The first is *the gift of realism*. The book of Esther reminds us of the ongoing reality of evil in this world, evil which is often expressed in the persecution of God's people.

We can't go very far into this book before we meet one of the most unsavory, despicable human beings to ever occupy the human stage. His name? Haman!

This man was appointed by King Ahasuerus of Persia to

serve as his prime minister. He, Haman, would be second only to the king himself in terms of power and authority.

Here we have a glaring example of the terrible results of putting bad people into high offices.

The mistake of appointing the vile Haman was bad enough, but the king made it worse by commanding all the citizens to bow when Haman walked by. One man refused to comply—a Jew named Mordecai. Here now is the vileness of Haman: because Mordecai refused to bow before him, Haman hatched a plot to have Mordecai and all the Jews of Persia executed. He went to the king to have this plot approved, and the king, making yet another horrible mistake, granted Haman's request.

What reason did Haman give for wanting the Jews exterminated? They were different (Est. 3:8).

Persecution of Christians is growing exponentially around the world. The reason? Oftentimes, it is that they, by virtue of their convictions, cannot go along with political correctness. They're different.

The book of Esther doesn't sugarcoat things. It tells us to expect to encounter the evils of hatred and persecution. It tells us to be realistic.

A second gift from Esther is *the gift of assurance.*

One of the unusual things about this book is that it doesn't mention God. But while His name isn't here, He is here. He is here to overrule evil and to care for His people. In troubling and threatening times, we need nothing more than this calm assurance: God is at work even when He seems not to be, and the work He is doing is for the glory of His name and the good of His people.

Undiscerning people will read Esther and marvel at the sequence of unlikely events. They will call them "coincidences." They are actually "providences," that is, God guiding events to accomplish His purposes. It was the guiding hand of God that brought Esther to the throne, that brought about the execution of the hateful Haman, and that delivered the Jews.

But the best gift Esther gives us is *the gift of Christ*. Christ in the book of Esther? Absolutely!

What we have in this book is God working through a mediator (Esther) to save His people from the sentence of death.

A mediator is a go-between. To save her people, Esther stepped between the one who had issued the death decree (the king) and her people. She pleaded with the king on behalf of her people, and the king issued another decree that effectively spared the Jews.

The Lord Jesus is the mediator between God and sinners. God has handed down the sentence of eternal destruction on all of us as the just penalty for our sins. But Jesus stepped between us and that decree. He received the wrath that decree demands so all who believe in Him will never have to endure that wrath themselves.

So the greatest gift of the book of Esther is that it points us to One greater than Esther. While we thank God for her, we thank Him even more for Jesus.

# -5-

# From God's Word, the Bible...

*I am like a pelican of the wilderness;*
*I am like an owl of the desert.*
*I lie awake,*
*And am like a sparrow alone on the housetop.*

*Psalm 102:6-7*

# Which Bird Should I Be?

How often David must have been a bird-watcher! In Psalm 55:6, he mentions the dove, and in Psalm 102:6-7, the pelican, the owl, and the sparrow. (It's true that Psalm 102 does not identify him as its author, but it seems very much in the style of David.)

The pelican, owl, and sparrow represented David as he sometimes found himself to be. These birds are fitting emblems for loneliness. The pelican is away from his natural habitat and alone in the wilderness. The owl is alone in the desert. The sparrow sits alone on the housetop.

The pelican and the owl are also known for their soft moaning.

David could easily identify with those birds. He was so burdened and troubled that he felt all alone and went along softly moaning. And we have no trouble identifying with David. We know what it is to have what we might describe as the pelican problem. We sometimes feel utterly alone and helpless. Our hearts are so heavy that we moan as we go along. Our experience and burdens are such that the wilderness seems to be a fitting image for the world in which we live.

What was causing David to feel so burdened? It was the problem he so often expresses in the Psalms—his enemies. He writes in Psalm 102:8:

> *My enemies reproach me all day long;*
> *And those who deride me swear an oath against me.*

In Psalm 55, we find another instance of David moaning (v. 2) for the same reason—the hatred of his enemies (v. 3). On this occasion, he thought of another bird—the gentle, peaceful dove. That dove represented David as he often wished he could be. He writes yearningly in verse 6:

> *Oh, that I had wings like a dove!*
> *For then I would fly away and be at rest...*

Have you ever wished you could just fly away and "be at rest"? How often in these stress-filled times we hear someone say: "I need to get away from it for a while!" As we increasingly face the Christophobia of this time—the resistance to biblical Christianity—we might find ourselves longing to escape and find peace. Or it may simply be our personal pressures and responsibilities that make us feel that way.

There is yet another bird that represents David as he knew he should always be. While David doesn't specifically name that bird, we have no trouble identifying it. We are now in Psalm 57, and David's problem has once again raised its ugly head. There are people who would "swallow" him up (v. 3), individuals who were more like lions than people. They were ready to devour him (v. 4) and to entrap him (v.6).

So what bird came to David's mind on this occasion? It was not the dove. It was the little chick. David says to the Lord (v. 1):

*And in the shadow of Your wings I will make my refuge,*
*Until these calamities have passed by.*

When danger arises, the mother hen clucks and spreads her wings, and the little chicks immediately run under those wings and stay there until the danger has passed.

We might say David has traded wings! He has traded the wings of the dove for the wings of the mother hen. He realized that he didn't need *escaping* wings because he had in the Lord *sheltering* wings.

How do we run to God and find shelter? We must run to His Word. There is a "clucking" there. God warns us of danger and extends comfort to us in His Word, but it will be of no avail to us if we do not avail ourselves of it.

Then we must run to prayer. David writes (v. 2):

*I will cry out to God Most High,*
*To God who performs all things for me.*

And we run to God by running to praise, saying with David (vv. 7, 11):

*I will sing and give praise.*
*…Be exalted, O God, above the heavens;*
*Let Your glory be above all the earth.*

Which bird should I be? I, and you, should be like the little chick. When we feel like a pelican, we should not act like a dove; rather, we should learn to act like a chick taking refuge in the everlasting shelter of the wings of the Almighty.

# -6-

# From God's Word, the Bible...

*In those days Hezekiah was sick and near death, and he prayed to the LORD; and He spoke to him and gave him a sign. But Hezekiah did not repay according to the favor shown him, for his heart was lifted up; therefore wrath was looming over him and over Judah and Jerusalem. Then Hezekiah humbled himself for the pride of his heart, he and the inhabitants of Jerusalem, so that the wrath of the LORD did not come upon them in the days of Hezekiah.*

2 Chronicles 32:24-26

# The Worst Kind of Forgetfulness

Most of us wage an ongoing battle with forgetfulness. We find ourselves forgetting appointments, names, and faces. Most episodes of our forgetfulness are annoying but harmless. We forget where we put our keys and we are delayed for a few minutes. But no real damage is done. There are times, however, when forgetfulness can be very harmful indeed.

Meet Hezekiah, king of Judah. Here is a man who fell into the worst kind of forgetfulness, and it was anything but harmless. Here is a man who forgot to be grateful.

If there was ever a man who had lots of reasons to be thankful, it was Hezekiah. He and his kingdom had been delivered from the threat of being conquered by Sennacherib, the powerful king of Assyria (v. 22). In addition to that, the Lord had given Hezekiah prominence in the eyes of the surrounding nations (v. 23). Then there was that episode in which the Lord graciously promised to extend

Hezekiah's life by fifteen years (Isa. 38:5).

These are only three of the many, many blessings the Lord bestowed on Hezekiah. He was an abundantly blessed man, and, as such, he should have been abundantly thankful. And we expect to read that he was, but, shockingly enough, we read: "Hezekiah did not repay according to the favor shown him …" (v. 25).

There is no way anyone can ever repay God for blessings, but one can at the very least demonstrate his or her gratitude by truly worshiping Him (Heb. 13:15) and by obeying His commandments (Luke 6:46).

Hezekiah failed. Although he had been so signally blessed by God, he turned his back on Him. Why did he do it? His heart was "lifted up" with pride (v. 25).

There are plenty of thanksgiving-killers—being busy with responsibilities and pleasures, being occupied with the problems of life, failing to walk in close communion with the Lord. But there is no more prolific thanksgiving-killer than pride. Pride kills thanksgiving because it causes us to think we deserve what we receive. We are not grateful for things we deserve. They are owed to us, and it is only right and fair that we should have them.

We are grateful, however, for those things that are given to us without our deserving them. And here is the thing we so often lose sight of—we don't really deserve anything at all. Everything we have is given to us, not because we deserve it, but rather because of the goodness and grace of God.

Hezekiah emerges from the pages of Scripture as a reminder to be careful about thanksgiving. Every child of God can and should join the psalmist in saying:

> *Blessed be the LORD,*
> *Who daily loads us with benefits,*

*The God of our salvation.*
(Ps. 68:19)

God has, as it were, loaded the wagons of our lives with the bounty of heaven. What do we consider to be good? Family? Health? Friends? Material wellbeing? All come from God (James 1:17).

In addition to these things, the children of God have received the most wonderful blessing the Lord has to bestow—forgiveness for sin and eternal life through the redeeming work of Jesus.

Who can calculate the greatness of this? The Second Person of the Trinity, who was fully God, left the glories of heaven and came to this earth in our humanity. He rendered perfect obedience to God, thus providing for sinners the righteousness they need to stand acceptably before God. Then He went to the cross to actually receive the wrath of God, thus paying the penalty our sins deserve. Christianity in a nutshell is this—He got our sins and we get His righteousness (2 Cor. 5:21).

What a blessing! And all are invited to come and receive what Christ has done.

If we have received it, gratitude should reign in our lives. We must not forget what God has done for us in Christ. No Christian can forget forever, but to even forget for a while is the worst kind of forgetfulness.

# －7－

# From God's Word, the Bible...

*Offer to God thanksgiving,
And pay your vows to the Most High.*

*Psalm 50:1*

*...bearing with one another, and forgiving one another, if anyone
has a complaint against another; even as Christ forgave you,
so you also must do.*

*Colossians 3:13*

# Reminders from Molly

The Bible tells us to consider the ant (Prov. 6:6) and to look at the birds (Matt. 6:26). It points us to the ox and the donkey (Isa. 1:3) and also to the deer (Ps. 42:1). So it is obvious that animals can teach us vital and valuable lessons.

My wife and I have a dog named Molly. Molly is a Morkie: half Maltese, half Yorkie.

Molly has many qualities that I admire, and a few, well, not so much.

One of Molly's admirable traits is gratitude.

Every time we eat a meal, I feed Molly a few morsels. After the meal is over, I usually sit in my easy chair. Invariably, Molly jumps on my lap and begins to lick my face and wag her tail. I'm sure it's her way of expressing gratitude to me for sharing my food with her.

I learned as a child the importance of gratitude, but I need to be reminded. Molly reminds me. I think she knows that I will continue to take care of her even if she doesn't express gratitude. But she can't help herself. Gratitude is so much a part of her nature that she has to express it. She is rich in gratitude.

We need to work hard to make sure we are grateful for God's greatest blessing—salvation through His Son, the Lord Jesus. That should daily fill our hearts and call forth our praise. But being thankful for that blessing does not fully discharge our responsibility. We are to be thankful for all of God's blessings. Paul urges us to be "…giving thanks always for all things to God the Father in the name of our Lord Jesus Christ…" (Eph. 5:20). In 1 Thessalonians 5:18, he adds: "…in everything give thanks, for this is the will of God in Christ Jesus for you."

"For" and "in" are little words with large meaning! Be thankful for all things and in all things.

Let's get back to Molly. She also reminds me that failure doesn't have to be final. A good bit of each day for Molly is sitting on our back porch watching for squirrels to come into our fenced yard. They do come often to eat the seeds that fall to the ground from our bird feeder. When a squirrel arrives, Molly immediately goes into her stalking mode. Inching forward ever so slightly, she imagines each time that she will finally catch the elusive squirrel. She never does. But that doesn't keep her from trying. She refuses to accept failure as final.

We fail in our Christian walk many times, and the devil is ever anxious to assure us that our failures are so severe that the Lord wants nothing more to do with us. But failure is not final for the Christian. Simon Peter failed miserably when he denied the Lord three times, but the Lord was not through with him. When we fail, we must not lie down in our failure but ask the Lord to forgive us and start moving forward again.

Molly also reminds me to be a quick-forgiver. Molly does

not have a doghouse, but she sometimes gets in the doghouse, if you know what I mean. Although she has to be rebuked and corrected, she doesn't hold it against my wife or me. And she doesn't hold it against us when we take her to the veterinarian. She forgets and forgives quickly.

The Bible calls all believers not to nurse resentment and bitterness but to forgive. Paul writes: "And be kind to one another, tenderhearted, forgiving one another, just as God in Christ also forgave you" (Eph. 4:32).

Most of all Molly reminds me of the importance of love and trust. She loves us unconditionally and she trusts us to do what is good and right for her. Every Christian loves the Lord, and every Christian trusts the Lord. But love and trust are always matters of degree. They do not always stay the same. They fluctuate and vacillate. Molly's love for me and trust in me seem to be unchanging. They are always at the same high level.

I need to be more like Molly.

# -8-

# From God's Word, the Bible...

*So Elijah went to present himself to Ahab; and there was a severe famine in Samaria. And Ahab had called Obadiah, who was in charge of his house. (Now Obadiah feared the LORD greatly. For so it was, while Jezebel massacred the prophets of the LORD, that Obadiah had taken one hundred prophets and hidden them, fifty to a cave, and had fed them with bread and water.) And Ahab had said to Obadiah, "Go into the land to all the springs of water and to all the brooks; perhaps we may find grass to keep the horses and mules alive, so that we will not have to kill any livestock." So they divided the land between them to explore it; Ahab went one way by himself, and Obadiah went another way by himself.*

*From 1 Kings 18:1-16*

# Mr. Debatable

Who is Mr. Debatable? It is none other than Obadiah, the servant of the extremely vile and wicked King Ahab.

I call him Mr. Debatable because students of the Bible are divided on whether he is a man to be commended or one to be condemned. I lean toward the former. My summary of Obadiah goes like this: in tough times he was a good man who had moments of weakness.

Tough times? Without a doubt! It was the time when Ahab and Jezebel ruled the nation of Israel.

A little bit now about Jezebel; she was a Sidonian who came into her marriage to Ahab with a radical commitment to the god Baal. Baal was a nature god. He supposedly controlled the weather and thus secured for his devotees the fertility of the land and an abundant harvest.

Her husband, Ahab, may very well have been more of a syncretist or synthesist, that is, he may have thought that he could synthesize or blend the worship of Baal with the worship of God. Jezebel was no synthesist. She was all out for Baal. It was Baal or nothing in her book.

We may find it hard to believe, but Baal worship by this time had grown so much that it had almost taken over Israel. A nation so immensely blessed by God had now set God aside.

This was also the time of the prophet Elijah. He is the one who came storming into Ahab's presence to announce that there would be no rain in Israel until he, Elijah, said so.

Three-and-a-half years passed, and there had not been a drop of rain. So much for Baal controlling the weather!

Now back to Mr. Debatable! During those exceedingly difficult times, Obadiah performed admirably. Jezebel was out to kill every prophet of the Lord, but Obadiah, at the risk of losing his life, hid one hundred of them and sustained them with food and water. Where did he get the water in this time of drought? We do not know.

If Obadiah performed so heroically, what is so debatable about him? It's because he had some moments of weakness when Elijah suddenly showed up and asked him to arrange a meeting with Ahab. Obadiah began to waver. He feared for his life. He thought he would get the meeting arranged, Elijah would again disappear, and he, Obadiah, would be executed on the spot. Obadiah wavered when the chips were down, much like Simon Peter would do centuries later when he denied the Lord Jesus three times.

But Obadiah's wavering was temporary. The Word of the Lord was confronting him through Elijah. Obadiah initially preferred that the Word work apart from his own involvement, and he had no trouble coming up with an excuse. But the Word continued to press upon him until it won his heart. The Word pressed and pressed until it overcame his reluctance and halfheartedness and propelled him into obedience. So we read these blessed words: "So Obadiah went to meet Ahab, and told him; and Ahab went to meet Elijah" (v. 16).

Let's picture Elijah as the representative of the Word of God and Obadiah as the representative of the people of God. In Elijah's command to Obadiah to go to Ahab, we have God's Word taking hold of God's people and pressing them into service.

God's Word still does that. It still speaks to God's people. We can so easily be like Obadiah. We can desire for the Word to do its work while we sit on the sidelines and cheer. It's so very easy for us to want the Lord to address the Ahabs of this world without addressing us.

We need revival. In times of revival, the first thing the Lord does is address His own people (2 Chron. 7:14). He calls upon them to repudiate and renounce their halfheartedness and their desire for private discipleship so that they can be channels for His holy Word.

Was Obadiah's performance debatable? No more than the performance of God's people today! Isn't it good to know that the God who did not give up on him does not give up on us?

# -9-

## From God's Word, the Bible...

*For such are false apostles, deceitful workers, transforming themselves into apostles of Christ. And no wonder! For Satan himself transforms himself into an angel of light. Therefore it is no great thing if his ministers also transform themselves into ministers of righteousness, whose end will be according to their works.*

2 Corinthians 11:13-15

*(Also read Mark 4:1-20 for this meditation.)*

# Does the Devil Go to Church?

Let's not be in doubt about the existence of the devil. He is a real person. He started out as one of God's angels, perhaps even the greatest among the angels. But he became full of himself and actually thought that he could be God. So he persuaded other angels to join him in an attempt to defeat and dethrone God. But it didn't work—rebellion against God never does—and he and his angels were cast out of heaven. So Lucifer ("morning star" or, more literally, "son of the morning")—that was his original name—became Satan. The name Satan means "adversary." As the name suggests, Satan's grand scheme is to oppose God.

Let's turn our attention to the church of the Lord Jesus. There is so very much that we could say about her, but at this point we should focus on one thing in particular—the church's special connection to the truth of God. The Apostle Paul calls her "the pillar and ground of the truth" (1 Tim. 3:15). As pillars and foundations hold up or support a building, so the church is to uphold and support the truth of God's Word and, more particularly, the truth of the gospel.

The church is to love, support, and exalt the truth of God. She is to rejoice when the truth is held high, and mourn when the truth is cast down into the mire.

The devil hates the truth of God with the utmost hatred. He labors to undermine, defeat, and destroy it.

Now to our question—does the devil go to church? That depends. There is no need for him to attend churches that have no interest in God's truth. There is no work for him to do in such churches. The work is already done. Such churches are not really churches. They have the name, but that is all.

There are churches that the devil loves to attend—Bible-believing, Bible-preaching churches in which Christ is exalted. It is hard to get people to attend such churches, but Satan never misses a service.

It would seem that the devil would stay away from such services. Why would he expose himself to the truth that he so hates? J.C. Ryle writes of Satan:

> ...nowhere perhaps is the devil so active as in a congregation of Gospel-hearers.... From him come wandering thoughts and roving imaginations,–listless minds and dull memories,—sleepy eyes and fidgety nerves,—weary ears and distracted attention. ...We shall always find him at Church. He never stays away from public ordinances. Let us remember this, and be upon our guard.[1]

If we think this sounds fanciful and far-fetched, we need

---

[1] *Expository Thoughts on Luke, vol. i*, The Banner of Truth Trust, Edinburgh, 1986, pp. 250-1

to revisit Jesus' parable of the sower. The sower goes out to his field to sow his seed. The seed would be God's Word, and the sower the preacher. As the sower sows, the seed falls on various types of ground—"wayside" ground, stony ground, thorny ground, and good ground. These represent the hearers. Of the "wayside" hearers, Jesus says: "And when they hear, Satan comes immediately and takes away the word that was sown in their hearts" (Mark 4:15).

Amazingly enough, Satan may even attend church as the preacher. The Apostle Paul says: "…Satan himself transforms himself into an angel of light. Therefore it is no great thing if his ministers also transform themselves into ministers of righteousness, whose end will be according to their works" (2 Cor. 11:14-15).

Satan at church! In the pulpit and in the pew! What a sobering thought! Let's make sure we keep our wits about us even while we are in church, and let's seek to love and support the truth as much as Satan hates and opposes it.

# -10-

## From God's Word, the Bible...

*"Fear not, you worm Jacob,*
*You men of Israel!*
*I will help you," says the LORD*
*And your Redeemer, the Holy One of Israel.*
*"Behold, I will make you into a new threshing sledge with sharp teeth;*
*You shall thresh the mountains and beat them small,*
*And make the hills like chaff.*
*You shall winnow them, the wind shall carry them away,*
*And the whirlwind shall scatter them;*
*You shall rejoice in the LORD,*
*And glory in the Holy One of Israel."*

*Isaiah 41:14-16*

# The Worm Crushing the Mountain

Worms are lowly, helpless little creatures, and mountains are majestic and mighty. What we have in these verses, then, is the promise that the lowly and helpless will destroy the mighty and majestic.

We could easily dismiss this as lunacy if it were not for the fact that it was the Lord who promised this, and it has already come true.

The worm in this passage refers to God's people. The Lord says:

> *Fear not, you worm, Jacob,*
> *You men of Israel!*

The mountains refer to the difficulties facing God's people at that time. It was a most challenging and serious time. The people of God had seemingly lost everything. Their homes and cities lay in ruins, their temple was demolished, and they themselves were captives in distant Babylon.

Babylon was so very powerful, and the Jews so very weak. If we had been there to observe and to give odds on the Jews returning home from Babylon, we might have said: "It would be about the same odds as a worm crushing a mountain!"

But that worm did crush that mountain. Babylon was defeated, and the Jews returned home. It was not because the weak Jews suddenly became powerful. It was all God's doing. The Lord had promised to help them (v. 14), and help them He did. He raised up the Persians to defeat Babylon, and He put it into the heart of the Persian king, Cyrus, to release the Jews.

The church today seems very much like a worm in the face of an increasingly anti-Christian world. Where is her hope? It's in the Lord who can cause worms to level mountains. He has helped His church in the past, and He still has the ability to help her today. He has promised that the gates of hell will not prevail against her (Matt. 16:18).

There is also encouragement in this passage for individual believers who are facing hardships. Our God is a helping God! He may not help us as quickly as we would like. (The Jews were in captivity for seventy years before they were released.) And He may not help us in the ways that we would like. But we must never doubt that God helps His people.

Believers were once facing the largest of all difficulties. We were in our sins and under the righteous condemnation of God. We were part of Satan's domain and facing the wrath of God. We had no more chance of overcoming these difficulties than a worm has of crushing a mountain.

But our helping God stepped in! He who identifies Himself as the "Redeemer" (v. 14) has redeemed us. He has taken us out of our sins and given us eternal life.

How did God accomplish this for us? The answer is written large in Scripture. It was through His Son, the Lord Jesus Christ. More specifically, it was through His Son going to the cross to die in our stead. On that cross, Jesus received the wrath of God so all who believe in Him would never have to receive that wrath themselves.

We find in Psalm 22 a detailed anticipation of Jesus' death on the cross. It is essentially the Lord Jesus Himself describing His death centuries before it occurred. At one point, He cries:

> *But I am a worm, and no man;*
> *A reproach of men, and despised of the people.*
> (Ps. 22:6)

Our ability to deal with our sins was on a par with the ability of a worm to crush a mountain, but Jesus became a worm in our stead and crushed for us the mountain of condemnation.

When our circumstances are harsh, let's remember that God has already helped us by doing for us the greatest thing He could do. He has provided salvation for us. If God has already helped us in that way, we may rest assured that He will help us in every other situation.

The redeeming work of God will one day culminate in His people leaving this realm of tears and coming into eternal glory. We will most certainly be amazed that we are there, and we will be keenly aware that we do not deserve to be there. And when we hear one of our fellow-saints say: "Isn't this amazing?" we may be inclined to answer: "Yes, it's like worms crushing mountains."

# -11-

# From God's Word, the Bible...

*Look now at the behemoth, which I made along with you;*
*He eats grass like an ox.*

*Job 40:15*

# Look to the Hippo

Job was deeply devoted to the Lord. He was also a very prosperous man. One day Satan came before the Lord to discuss Job. Satan suggested that Job was faithful to God because He had so abundantly blessed him. If the Lord were to withdraw His blessings, Satan argued, Job would immediately turn against Him.

The Lord took up the challenge. He gave Satan permission to remove Job's prosperity, and remove it Satan did. When he was through, Job was without children, herds, herdsmen, and health. All he had left was his wife and some friends, all of whom insisted on giving him bad advice.

Most of the book is taken up with that bad advice and with Job's response to it. The book comes to a close with the Lord Himself speaking to Job (38:1-41:34). God never tells Job about Satan's challenge and His response. He primarily asks Job a series of questions that are designed to point out His greatness. In the midst of these questions, the Lord tells Job to look at the "behemoth." This is a reference to a beast of some kind. Many commentators think it is the hippopotamus or even a dinosaur.

What an amazing thing! Job was suffering horribly, and yet God tells him to look at the hippo. This seems to be the totally inadequate answer of the adequate God.

Can you relate to this? Do you sometimes feel that God is giving you totally inadequate answers to the challenges and crises of life? Perhaps you are facing harsh difficulties, and when you look to God it seems as if He is telling you to look to the hippo!

We can be sure that God has the answers we need. There is nothing going on in our lives that He cannot explain. He knows why you or your family member is sick; He knows why your loved one died; He knows why this world is such a mess. You cannot possibly ask God a question that He cannot answer.

But the fact that God knows the answers doesn't mean that He shares them with us. God has often puzzled His people by doing things that didn't seem to make sense.

Here, then, is the question: why would God tell Job to look at a great creature such as a hippopotamus? The answer would seem to be that it takes more wisdom and power to make a hippopotamus than we realize. The Lord intended that Job would draw this conclusion: if God had enough wisdom and power to make a hippo, He had enough wisdom and power to govern Job's life.

Job's responsibility in the midst of his searing adversity was not to question God but rather to bow before His wisdom and power. And God's call to Job is His call to us. When the circumstances of life seem to be too difficult for us, we must always remember that there is a divine wisdom at work in our circumstances.

Here now is a man hanging on a Roman cross outside Jerusalem, and God points to that cross and tells us that the only way our sins can be forgiven is through that man hanging on that cross. He tells us that man is not dying there as other men died on other crosses. He died a special kind of death. He actually received an eternity's worth of the wrath of God in the place of sinners. If we want to be delivered from that wrath, we must repent of our sins and accept from our hearts what that man did on that cross.

A man dying on a cross 2,000 years ago is the way of salvation? It seems so inadequate. Laden down with the guilt of our sins, we come to God, and He points us to that cross. It seems as if He is mocking us. We have this horrible problem, and He tells us to look to the hippo! But God's wisdom and power are in that cross (1 Cor. 1:18-25), and if we are to be saved we must bow before it.

Look to the hippo; and, once you have looked to the hippo, look beyond and up to the man God appointed—the man Christ Jesus—whose saving work on the cross is sufficient for needy sinners such as we all are.

# -12-

## From God's Word, the Bible...

*Will the Lord cast off forever?*
*And will He be favorable no more?*
*Has His mercy ceased forever?*
*Has His promise failed forevermore?*
*Has God forgotten to be gracious?*
*Has He in anger shut up His tender mercies? Selah*
*And I said, "This is my anguish;*
*But I will remember the years of the right hand of the Most High."*
*I will remember the works of the LORD;*
*Surely I will remember Your wonders of old.*
*I will also meditate on all Your work,*
*And talk of Your deeds.*

*Psalm 77:7-12*

# Searching Questions from a Miserable Man

What was it anyway? What was causing Asaph, the author of this psalm, to be so miserable?

He was miserable. There can be no doubt about that. In verse 2 he mentions the day of his trouble. In the same verse he says this trouble was so deep and serious that his soul refused to be comforted.

In verse 3 he tells us that even the thought of God did not bring him any comfort. He also indicates that his spirit was overwhelmed. In verse 4, he says he couldn't sleep. He also tells us that he couldn't even talk about his trouble. Most of us find relief by being able to share our troubles with our friends, but not Asaph.

Had he wrecked his new chariot? Was he facing an audit from the tax authorities? Had his favorite team lost an important game?

Are you ready for this? Asaph tells us that his misery came from considering the past:

*I have considered the days of old,*
*The years of ancient times.*
(v. 5)

Why did he find the past to be so troubling? Was there some great, glaring failure there that now raised its ugly head to fill him with regret and guilt? Not at all! The past he was considering was good. It was one in which he had a song in the night (v. 6).

Why would a good past vex him and make him so miserable? It made him realize that his present couldn't begin to compare to that wonderful past. Asaph was in trouble because he could look at the past and see marvelous instances of God at work in his life and in the lives of those around him. But the present was such that there were no such instances or evidences of God at work.

As you view your present situation, maybe like Asaph you feel in your experience and circumstances as if

- God has cast you off forever and God has decided to be favorable to you no more (see v. 7)
- God's mercy has ceased forever and God's promise has failed (see v. 8)
- God has forgotten to be gracious and God in anger has locked up all His tender mercies and thrown away the key (see v. 9).

Asaph was in a terrible state because the people of God had enjoyed a glorious past? Really? That seems bizarre, but that is exactly what Asaph tells us. He says:

*This is my anguish.*
(v. 10)

Anguish is not the final word for Asaph. There in verse 10 he also turns the corner. As he reflected on the glories of the past, he suddenly realized that he had been looking at them in the wrong way. Instead of letting those glories depress him, he should have been letting them bless him. The fact that God had worked so mightily in the past meant that there was hope for the future. The God of the past hasn't changed. He is still the same, and, no matter how bleak and dreary our circumstances are, they are not greater than our God. He can break in and do glorious things today even as He did in bygone days.

Asaph's account of his bout with despondency forces us to ask ourselves some very penetrating and searching questions:

- Are we as concerned about the current condition of the people of God as Asaph was? If not, why not? There is certainly plenty to be concerned about.
- What are we doing about the current situation? Are we crying to God regarding it? Are we seeking His face, or have we fallen into the trap of merely lamenting the situation?
- Are we assuming that it is impossible for us to see a mighty moving of God's Spirit, that such a moving is a thing of the past and cannot be repeated? Do we think that the times in which we live are too hard for God? Or are we letting the fact that God has moved powerfully in the past to encourage us to believe that He can move powerfully again?

May the experience of Asaph encourage us to lay hold of God in prayer—and as a result, may we live well for Him in the grace of the gospel of the Lord Jesus Christ.

# -13-

# From God's Word, the Bible...

*No one calls for justice,*
*Nor does any plead for truth.*
*They trust in empty words and speak lies;*
*They conceive evil and bring forth iniquity.*
*They hatch vipers' eggs and weave the spider's web;*
*He who eats of their eggs dies,*
*And from that which is crushed a viper breaks out.*

*We all growl like bears,*
*And moan sadly like doves;*
*We look for justice, but there is none;*
*For salvation, but it is far from us.*

*Isaiah 59:4-5, 11*
*See also Isaiah 59:20.*

# Should You Growl Like a Bear?

One day the Spirit of God tapped the prophet Isaiah on the shoulder and said: "I want you to hear something." So the prophet leaned over, put his ear on the windowpane of the future and listened intently. And what did he hear? Growling and moaning! More precisely, he heard the growling of bears and the moaning of doves. The growling was the sound of angry complaining, while the moaning was the sound of sadness.

Where would all this growling and moaning come from? It would come from Isaiah's people, the people of Judah. And when would it occur? Several years after Isaiah died! What would cause it? Their captivity in Babylon!

Bears growl when they are impatient for food, and there in Babylon the people would be impatient with God. They did, after all, consider themselves to be the people of God. Shouldn't that have translated into blessing instead of adversity? Do people who profess faith in God not have the right to expect His protection and care? But Isaiah's people would be experiencing problems, and there would seem to be no end in sight.

Would the people of Judah have a right to growl and moan in their time of captivity? Would they have reason to complain about God?

As Isaiah drew away from the windowpane of the future, the Spirit of God said to him: "I want you to write down the truth of the matter now. When the people begin to growl and moan in their captivity, they will be able to read what you write and the record will be set straight."

What did the Spirit want Isaiah to write? It was not a message that the people of Judah would want to hear, but it did set the record straight. The reason the people would be growling like bears in Babylon is because of their hatching of vipers' eggs and their weaving of spiders' webs (v. 5).

In other words, the people of Judah would have no reason to complain against God in their captivity because they themselves would be responsible for it. Their captivity would come about because of their nurturing of things that they should have destroyed.

If you were to find vipers' eggs in your backyard, what would you do? You certainly wouldn't hatch them and cuddle the vipers. You would destroy those eggs before the vipers hatched to destroy you.

For years and years, the people of Judah had nurtured things they should have destroyed. They had nurtured idolatry and immorality. God sent them prophet after prophet to urge them to destroy those things, but they refused to listen. When they finally ended up in captivity, they had no one to blame but themselves. To change the figure, they had woven for themselves a spider's web, and the captivity would be nothing more than them being trapped in the very web that they had woven.

The sad truth is that even in their captivity they continued for some time to cuddle their vipers before finally coming to their senses and turning back to God.

What about us? Are we nurturing things that will destroy us if we don't destroy them?

The Lord is ever kind to His people—even when He seems not to be kind. So the Spirit of God prompted Isaiah to include a marvelous note of hope. We might say the Spirit refused to leave them growling like bears.

Yes, the captivity would come about because of their bad choices, and, yes, it would be a difficult time. It would often seem to them as if God had totally abandoned them. But there was no cause for despair. God would come to them if they would sincerely turn from their sins in true repentance:

*"The Redeemer will come to Zion,*
*And to those who turn from transgression in Jacob,"*
*Says the LORD.*
(Isa. 59: 20)

What a marvelous message the Bible contains! It tells us that God can and does forgive those who have been so foolish as to hatch vipers' eggs. He can and does forgive on the basis of what Jesus did. He is the Redeemer promised in the above verse. The question is not whether God can forgive. It is, rather, whether we will repent.

# -14-

# From God's Word, the Bible...

*For thus says the LORD: After seventy years are completed at Babylon, I will visit you and perform My good word toward you, and cause you to return to this place. For I know the thoughts that I think toward you, says the LORD, thoughts of peace and not of evil, to give you a future and a hope. Then you will call upon Me and go and pray to Me, and I will listen to you. And you will seek Me and find Me, when you search for Me with all your heart.*

*Jeremiah 29:10-13*

# Where to Turn in Times of Trouble

In 597 BC the Babylonians invaded the land of Judah and carried 3,023 citizens into captivity. This group included King Jehoiachin, his household, and some priests and prophets. The same Babylonians would return eleven years later and completely destroy Jerusalem and take practically all the remaining inhabitants into captivity.

After the initial captivity in 597 BC, word reached Jeremiah that some of the prophets who had been taken were predicting that Babylon would collapse soon and that there would be a speedy release for the captives.

When Jeremiah heard this, he wrote a letter to tell the captives that the captivity would last for at least seventy years (v. 10).

Jeremiah's letter must have come as a crushing blow for them. Their hope for a quick return wasn't to be. So what was left? Jeremiah's letter also gave them the answer to that question. He told them where to take refuge in those trou-

~ 69 ~

bled times. Because we have troubles of our own, Jeremiah's answers are valid for us as well.

*First*, we must *turn to the truth of God* (vv. 8-9). The prophets in Babylon were telling the captives the things they wanted to hear, but that did not make those things true.

We might say that this was an early example of "feel-good" religion. It made the people feel good, but it did no good.

This kind of religion continues to thrive. Many decide what church they will attend of the basis of whether it makes them feel good. If the pastor talks about sin, coming judgment, and Christ as the only way of salvation, they hurry away. It doesn't occur to them to ask whether the pastor is telling the truth. They don't understand the purpose of religion that disturbs. It is for their good, just as it's for the good of the patient when the doctor tells him disturbing medical news.

*Secondly*, we must *turn to the thoughts of God* (v. 11).

Isn't it comforting to know that the Lord thinks about His people? The captives in Babylon must have thought the Lord had forgotten about them. This wasn't the case. The Lord says: "I know the thoughts that I think toward you."

Isn't it comforting to know that God has thoughts of peace about His people? The captives may have been saying: "Yes, God is thinking about us. He is thinking of ways to make us miserable."

But God told them it was not so. His thoughts were of "peace and not of evil." When God chastises His people, it isn't because He is mean and cruel but rather because He is kind and loving, and wants what is best for them.

Isn't it comforting to know that God thinks about the future?

God wanted the captives to know He had their future planned. Although the captivity wouldn't be short, it would definitely come to an end. When it did, God would restore them to their homeland.

Chastisement is never God's final word for His people. He chastises us to develop and mature us. Some day that process will be over, and God will bring us home to heaven.

Isn't it comforting to know that God's thinking about us can't be thwarted? The Jewish people were released from captivity just as the Lord promised, and all the promises He has regarding us will come true (Num. 23:19; Josh. 21:45).

*Finally*, our times of trouble should cause us to *turn to the throne of God* (vv. 12-13).

After promising to bring His people home, the Lord says: "Then you will call upon Me, and I will listen to you."

The word "then" doesn't refer to the time of their return home but rather to that time when the truth the Lord had just stated would come home to their hearts. In other words, when they realized that God was thinking about them and that He was thinking about their peace and about their future, they would then turn to Him in prayer. Knowing these things will surely drive us to prayer as well.

Are you troubled? Don't be. Take your troubles to the truth, the thoughts, and the throne of God; and then watch them melt away.

# -15-

# From God's Word, the Bible...

*"Let not your heart be troubled; you believe in God, believe also in Me. In My Father's house are many mansions; if it were not so, I would have told you. I go to prepare a place for you. And if I go and prepare a place for you, I will come again and receive you to Myself; that where I am, there you may be also. And where I go you know, and the way you know."*

*Thomas said to Him, "Lord, we do not know where You are going, and how can we know the way?"*

*Jesus said to him, "I am the way, the truth, and the life. No one comes to the Father except through Me."*

*John 14:1-6*

# A Place and a Peace

Chapters 13 through 16 of John's Gospel are immeasurably precious to the people of God. They relate some of what Jesus said to His disciples on the night before He was crucified. Someone observed that dying words are sacred words, and the words of these chapters can well be called the dying words of Jesus. The cross is now scant hours away.

Jesus had told His disciples on previous occasions that He must be put to death. But on those occasions His words seemed distant and unreal. On this night, it was all painfully real, and the disciples were crushed with sorrow.

So we aren't surprised to read that Jesus twice urged them not to let their hearts be troubled (John 14:1,27). The first time He used those words was in connection with a *place*, and the second in connection with a *peace*. So Jesus was saying that there was no reason for them to be troubled and distraught because they had a place to go and a peace until they got there. What He said to those despondent men applies equally to Christians today. We have a place to go, and we can enjoy peace while we are on the journey.

The place that awaits us is described by Jesus as "My Father's House" (John 14:1).

The Father's House! That means it is home, and that means it is the place of love, warmth, security, and pleasure.

Heaven is the Christian's home, and that we must never forget. We always get into trouble when we try to make this world our home. Good old Matthew Henry used to say this world is a traveling place and not a stopping place. The little rural church in which I grew up would often have the children sing this chorus:

> *This world is not my home*
> *I'm just a-passing though,*
> *My treasures are laid up*
> *Somewhere beyond the blue;*
> *The angels beckon me*
> *From heaven's open door,*
> *And I can't feel at home*
> *In this world anymore.*

The Father's house, Jesus said, is the place of many mansions. We associate mansions with permanence. Here is how permanent the Father's House is: it lasts forever!

One of the disciples, Thomas, must have been saying to himself: "The Father's house! That sounds wonderful! If only we knew the way to get there!" Then he blurted it out: "…how can we know the way?"

Jesus replied: "I am the way, the truth, and the life. No one comes to the Father except through Me."

To get to the Father's house, we have to come to the Father, and to come to the Father, we have to come to Jesus. He, Jesus, is the One who said: "I go to prepare a place for you" (v. 2).

Some understand Jesus to be saying that He was going back to heaven, and there He would busy Himself with building mansions. They imagine Him running around heaven with blueprints, hammers, saws, and nails. But Jesus was talking about going to the cross. That is where He dealt with the thing that keeps us out of heaven—sin! On the cross, He paid its penalty, and, in so doing, flung the door of heaven open wide to all who trust in Him and in what He did on that cross. On the basis of His work on that cross, Jesus is in heaven today to make intercession for all those who come to God through Him (Heb. 7:25).

So Christians have a place to go, but they also have a peace while they wait to get to the place. Jesus promised to give His peace to His disciples (v. 27).

This world cannot give us peace. It holds before us pleasures, possessions, and positions of influence and says: "These things will give you peace."

But it is all an illusion. Real peace is spiritual peace. It is peace that comes from knowing one is right with God in this world and will be present with Him in the world to come. The world may wish us peace, but it can never give us this kind of peace. Spiritual peace comes only through faith in the redeeming work of the Lord Jesus Christ and in being in a right relationship with Him.

# -16-

## From God's Word, the Bible...

*It is the Spirit who gives life; the flesh profits nothing. The words that I speak to you are spirit, and they are life.*

*John 6:63*

# The Words of Jesus

We have the words of many people from ancient times and countless words from countless people since those times. Some of these words are interesting and valuable; others are trivial and meaningless. Why give special attention to the words of Jesus? Why pay more attention to them than to the words of Aristotle, Plato, Socrates, Shakespeare or Mohammed?

The first reason is Jesus was a person like no other.

We frequently encounter the view that all religions are virtually the same, that one can be exchanged for another without any appreciable loss or gain. People who hold this view are astounded that Christians claim that Jesus alone is Lord and Savior. And oftentimes they are eager to dismiss us as biased fools.

Why do Christians hold this belief? The answer is, of course, the evidence that Jesus was precisely the person He claimed to be—God Himself in human flesh.

This assertion has been abundantly proven by:

- the miracles that Jesus performed

- the prophecies that He fulfilled
- His resurrection from the grave.

How do we know that these things occurred? They were recorded by men who either witnessed them or carefully researched them (Luke 1:1-4; John 1:14; 20:30-31; Acts 1:1-3; Heb. 2:3-4; 1 John 1:1-4). The words of Jesus, then, no matter how difficult and challenging they may be, must be heeded because they were spoken by the One who has been demonstrated to be the God-man.

We must go still further. We must pay attention to the words of Jesus because the very words themselves have a special quality about them. The people who heard Jesus speak testified to this (Matt. 7:28-29; 13:54; John 7:46).

Simon Peter gave testimony to this special power in an unforgettable way. After a huge multitude had decided that they could no longer follow Him, Jesus asked his original twelve disciples: "Do you also want to go away?" (John 6:67).

Simon responded: "Lord, to whom shall we go? You have the words of eternal life. Also we have come to believe and know that You are the Christ, the Son of the living God" (John 6:68-69).

Simon was echoing that which Jesus had spoken a moment earlier: "It is the Spirit who gives life; the flesh profits nothing. The words that I speak to you are spirit, and they are life" (John 6:63).

Simon agreed. He had heard in the words of Jesus the authentic ring of the way to eternal life.

Christians readily endorse what Simon Peter said. As we read the words of Jesus in Scripture, something within tells us that we are indeed reading special words, words that are genuine and true, and, yes, words that reveal the way to eternal life. And that way is the Lord Jesus Himself. When Jesus spoke about having eternal life, He spoke about the necessity of believing in Him (John 3:16; 5:39-40; 6:40,47).

As we connect the words of Jesus with eternal life, we can joyfully sing with Philip P. Bliss:

> *Christ, the blessed One, gives to all*
> *Wonderful words of life;*
> *Sinner, list to the loving call,*
> *Wonderful words of life;*
> *All so freely given,*
> *Wooing us to heaven.*
> *Beautiful words, wonderful words,*
> *Wonderful words of life;*
> *Beautiful words, wonderful words,*
> *Wonderful words of life.*

Yet another reason to pay special heed to the words of Jesus is this: those words have stood the test of time.

Each Sunday, and on other days as well, millions and millions of people gather together to study the words of Jesus. This is no small thing! Numberless authors have left the world with wonderful words. But only the words of Jesus receive attention on this scale week after week, not to mention the attention they receive from individuals on a daily basis. This must be considered a fulfillment of these words:

> *The grass withers, the flower fades,*
> *But the word of our God stands forever.*
> (Isa. 40:8)

The words of Jesus are in a category by themselves. No other words can begin to compare to them. Let us read them and heed them. If we do, we will land safely on heaven's shore, and there we will find that everything is just as He, Jesus, said (Luke 19:32; 22:13).

# -17-

# From God's Word, the Bible...

*But Zion said, "The LORD has forsaken me,*
*And my Lord has forgotten me."*
*"Can a woman forget her nursing child,*
*And not have compassion on the son of her womb?*
*Surely they may forget,*
*Yet I will not forget you.*
*See, I have inscribed you on the palms of My hands;*
*Your walls are continually before Me."*

*Isaiah 49:14-16*

# Quickly Forgotten, Forever Remembered

A college professor gives his new students a brief quiz. He first asks them to name their parents. Then he asks them to name their four grandparents. Finally, he asks them to name their eight great-grandparents.

As you would expect, the students have no trouble with the first two questions, but not one has been able to successfully answer the third.

Given these results, the professor concluded that we can expect our children and grandchildren to love us but our great grandchildren not to even know our names! So my five grandchildren are my last link to my being remembered in this world. How brief is our time on this earth and how brief is the remembrance of us when we are gone!

But for the Christian being forgotten in this world does not mean being totally forgotten. The Lord will always remember His people. Through His prophet Isaiah, the Lord said to His people:

> *Can a woman forget her nursing child,*
> *And not have compassion on the son of her womb?*
> *Surely they may forget,*
> *Yet I will not forget you.*
> (Isa. 49:15)

The people would receive these words during a terrible time of crisis. Because of their sins they would be in captivity in Babylon. That would put them five hundred miles away from Jerusalem, and the captivity would last a very long time—seventy years. But neither distance nor time could make the Lord forget them. He says to them:

> *See, I have inscribed you on the palms of My hands;*
> *Your walls are continually before Me.*
> (Isa. 49:16)

Just as it is impossible to forget the writing on the palms of our hands, so it is impossible for the Lord to forget His people. And this is no mere writing. The word "inscribed" means "engraved."

Didn't the Jews go into captivity because of sinful living? Yes. Were their sins not enough to cause God to completely forget them? No. Alexander Maclaren says: "…there is no sin that is strong enough to chill the divine love, or to erase us from the divine remembrance."[2]

And what about those walls? They refer to the walls of Jerusalem, and those walls were lying in ruins during those years of captivity. If someone had asked the Jewish captives there in Babylon to close their eyes and visualize the walls of Jerusalem, they would have said: "We see nothing but

---

[2] Alexander Maclaren, *Expositions of Holy Scripture: Isaiah and Jeremiah*, Baker Book House, Grand Rapids, 1974, p. 12

ruins." And they might very well have taken those ruins to mean that God had forgotten them. But where they saw ruins, God saw walls. Their sins, which had produced the ruins of Jerusalem, didn't mean that God had erased them from His memory. The fact that He saw future walls for Jerusalem meant He had not forgotten them

When the captivity came to an end (and it did come to an end, just as God promised), the Lord spoke to His people through the prophet Malachi. That would also be a time of great challenge. Wicked people would be so prospering and flourishing that it would cause the people of God to wonder if there was any point in serving the Lord (Mal. 2:17; 3:15). It would look as if God had forgotten to bless His faithful people and instead had chosen to bless the godless.

But God would not forget them. He keeps a book of remembrance that makes it impossible for Him to forget. In this world, His people are often treated with disdain. They are, as it were, thrown down into the mud to be trampled on. But in due time, God will pluck them out of the mire and will reveal them to be His precious jewels (Mal. 3:17). There is coming a day in which everyone will know that those who served the Lord in this life were wise to do so.

But how can we be sure that God never forgets His people? Let's go back to God having His people engraved on His hands. How can we be sure of this? We can be sure we are engraved on God's hands because of the hands of Jesus. God would never have allowed the hands of His Son to be nailed to the cross only to forget those who have trusted in Jesus and His redeeming death. Jesus' crucified hands are the proof that God's people are engraved on His hands.

Forgotten in this life? Very likely! Forgotten by God? Never!

# -18-

# From God's Word, the Bible...

*Now David was sitting between the two gates. And the watchman went up to the roof over the gate, to the wall, lifted his eyes and looked, and there was a man, running alone. Then the watchman cried out and told the king. And the king said, "If he is alone, there is news in his mouth." And he came rapidly and drew near. Then the watchman saw another man running, and the watchman called to the gatekeeper and said, "There is another man, running alone!" And the king said, "He also brings news."*

*From 2 Samuel 18:19-33*

# A Message from Ahimaaz

Ahimaaz could run. He wasn't just fast; he was very, very fast. If the Olympics had been in existence in his day, Ahimaaz would have been a gold medal winner in at least one event, and maybe in several.

It isn't surprising if you are having trouble remembering Ahimaaz. He isn't what we would call a major Bible character. He isn't in the same league as Abraham, Moses or David. He appears in only one chapter in the Bible, and only in the last half of that chapter. He falls into the category of obscure Bible characters.

Ahimaaz occupies such little space in the Bible that we might find ourselves wondering why he is even mentioned at all. The fact is, however, that he has a very important lesson to teach us. We might call him the minor man with a major message. What is that message? Let's wait for that.

Ahimaaz lived during that wretched time when King David's own son, Absalom, decided he wanted to be king.

That meant he would have to overthrow his father, but that didn't matter to Absalom who was a thoroughly disgusting human being.

So Absalom gathered a following—a large following—and tried to take the kingdom. It almost succeeded. But God made sure it didn't. Absalom's army was defeated, and he was slain. Joab, the captain of David's army, had to dispatch a runner to carry the news to David. At this point we meet Ahimaaz. He begged Joab to choose him, but Joab chose a man the Bible simply calls "the Cushite." The Cushite began running, and Ahimaaz continued begging until Joab, out of sheer exasperation, finally said: "Run" (v. 23).

That was the word Ahimaaz wanted to hear, and off he went. It didn't matter that the Cushite had a head start. Ahimaaz was fast. He passed the Cushite and got to David first with the news that the battle had been won. But David wanted to know more than the outcome of the battle. He wanted to know what had become of Absalom. Ahimaaz either couldn't say or he wouldn't say. Maybe he couldn't say. Maybe he, Ahimaaz, was telling the truth when he said to David: "I saw a great tumult, but I did not know what it was about" (v. 29). Joab had plainly said to Ahimaaz: "… the king's son is dead" (v. 20), but it's possible that the excitable Ahimaaz didn't even hear those words.

So Ahimaaz, the faster runner, had to stand alongside David until the slower runner, the Cushite, arrived with the news David most needed to hear—the news about his son. The Cushite put it in these words: "May the enemies of my lord the king, and all who rise against you to do you harm, be as that young man is!" (v. 32).

David understood. His son was dead.

And now we are ready for that vitally important message that Ahimaaz has to teach us. Ahimaaz didn't do well in his running to David, but he does run out of this narrative to deliver a message to us. In this running he does very well indeed. The message of Ahimaaz is this: it doesn't matter how fast we run if we don't deliver the message people most need to hear.

The Bible gives us a message we all need to hear. It tells us God has given us certain laws, and about our failure to keep those laws. Furthermore, it warns us about that day in which each of us must stand before God. If we stand there in our sins, we will be driven from Him. But the good news is that we don't have to stand before God in our sins. Through His Son, Jesus, God has done everything necessary for our sins to be forgiven. That forgiveness will be ours if we truly repent of our sins and trust in Christ.

This is the message churches and pastors are called to deliver, but, sadly enough, many, like Ahimaaz, are failing. They are running very fast and being very energetic in providing various activities and promotions, but, again, it doesn't matter how fast we run if we don't deliver the message people need.

I think Ahimaaz was warm, energetic, outgoing, and vibrant. I think I would like him; but when it comes to the matter of delivering the needed message, I don't want to be like him. Let me be like the Cushite.

# -19-

# From God's Word, the Bible...

*And when they crucified Him, they divided His garments, casting lots for them to determine what every man should take.*
*Now it was the third hour, and they crucified Him. And the inscription of His accusation was written above:*
*THE KING OF THE JEWS.*
*With Him they also crucified two robbers, one on His right and the other on His left. So the Scripture was fulfilled which says, "And He was numbered with the transgressors."*
*And those who passed by blasphemed Him, wagging their heads and saying, "Aha! You who destroy the temple and build it in three days, save Yourself, and come down from the cross!"*

*Mark 15:24-31*

# A Hymn Born in Heckling

The year was 1912. Evangelist George Bennard was preaching in a gospel crusade in Michigan. As he preached one night, he was continually heckled by a group of young people.

Shocked and deeply troubled by the contempt these young people expressed toward the gospel, Bennard wrote the first verse of *The Old Rugged Cross*:

> *On a hill far away*
> *Stood an old rugged cross*
> *The emblem of suffering and shame*
> *And I love that old cross*
> *Where the dearest and best*
> *For a world of lost sinners was slain.*

A few months later, Bennard added the last three verses of the hymn. In three of the four verses, he admits the disdain so many feel about the message of the cross. In verse one, the cross is the emblem of "shame." In verse two, it is "despised by the world." In verse four, it is the object of "shame and reproach."

With each of his candid acknowledgments of the world's hatred for the cross, Bennard gives a ringing affirmation of his esteem for it. In verse one, he says: "I love that old cross." In verse two, he declares that the cross holds "a wondrous attraction" for him. In verse three, he affirms that he sees "a wonderful beauty" in that cross. In verse four, he firmly resolves to "ever be true" to the cross and to "gladly bear" the "shame and reproach" connected with it.

In the chorus, he pledges to "cherish" the cross and to "cling" to it until that day on which he will "exchange it for a crown."

One writer understands Bennard to be suggesting that when believers get to heaven they will exchange what occurred on the cross so that they might receive a crown. Is this writer saying that believers in heaven will no longer need to think about the cross? I hope not!

That certainly is not what Bennard is saying. Rather he is declaring that in heaven, Christians will no longer have to endure the ridicule, the disdain, and the mockery that their love for the cross so often brings them in this life. In heaven they will finally exchange all of that for a crown. By the way, the "trophies" that Bennard says he will "lay down" refer to the scars and wounds he would receive in this life from those who despise the cross. Just as a soldier might consider his wounds to be "trophies" of war, so the Christian regards whatever wounds he receives for loving the cross not as wounds at all but rather as trophies. In heaven they will be laid down. No one in heaven will ever be wounded or scarred for loving the cross.

In heaven there will be no cross-haters, only cross-lovers

because everyone there will realize that he or she is there by virtue of that cross. In heaven believers will finally be all done with contempt for the cross and will wear the crown of victory.

It's not a good thing that Bennard was heckled so many years ago, but I'm glad that he was. That heckling prompted him to write a hymn that has brought tremendous blessing to millions.

Bennard certainly wasn't the first Christian to be heckled, and he wasn't the last. The heckling goes on today—with increasing intensity and ferocity, it seems. The more the hatred of the cross grows, the more we should appreciate Bennard's hymn. May God be pleased to use its words to instill in our hearts the fervent desire to "cherish" the cross and to "cling" to it! It will certainly be costly to do so, but we must be willing to pay the price, remembering all the while that Jesus paid a much greater price for us when He died on that cross.

*To the old rugged cross*
*I will ever be true,*
*Its shame and reproach gladly bear;*
*Then He'll call me someday*
*To my home far away,*
*Where His glory forever I'll share.*
*So I'll cherish the old rugged cross*
*Till my trophies at last I lay down;*
*I will cling to the old rugged cross*
*And exchange it some day for a crown.*

# -20-

# From God's Word, the Bible...

*A man who has friends must himself be friendly,*
*But there is a friend who sticks closer than a brother.*

*Proverbs 18:24*

*Greater love has no one than this, than to lay down one's life for his friends. You are My friends if you do whatever I command you. No longer do I call you servants, for a servant does not know what his master is doing; but I have called you friends, for all things that I heard from My Father I have made known to you.*

*From John 15:9-17*

# The Unfailing Friend

The *Andy Griffith Show* was produced in television's wholesome days. That was many years ago. In one episode, Andy, the sheriff of Mayberry, arrests a beautiful woman for speeding. It's obvious that she was not speeding a little but a lot. Barney, Floyd, and Opie were with Andy when the woman so flagrantly flaunted the law, but she so charmed them that they failed to give clear testimony regarding her violation. Opie's wavering could be forgiven. But there was no excuse for Barney and Floyd. At the end of the trial, Andy "congratulates" the woman for swaying the two men that he thought would "never leave" his side.

The episode ends well. The woman recognized that she had been wrong and paid her fine. And Andy's friendship with Barney and Floyd was repaired.

Most of us could write a similar script. We have to change the names and the circumstances, but the central plot—friend turning against friend—would remain the same. We know about this. We know about the pain it brings, and that pain is almost unbearable.

Experiencing the heartache of faithless friends should help us appreciate the friend who never fails. Who is that? Joseph M. Scriven supplies the answer:

> *What a friend we have in Jesus,*
> *All our sins and griefs to bear!*
> *What a privilege to carry,*
> *Everything to God in prayer!*

We know Scriven was no stranger to heartache. In 1845 he stood in stunned amazement as the body of his fiancée was lifted out of the murky waters of a lake. They were supposed to be married the next day.

In 1855 his mother was stricken with serious illness. Far from home and with no money to make the trip, Scriven wrote the lines of *What a Friend We Have in Jesus* and sent them to her.

In 1860 he lost another fiancée—this time to tuberculosis.

Two fiancées. Two deaths. A sick mother. I'd say Scriven knew about heartache. And evidently he also had friends turn against him. In the third verse he raises this question:

> *Do thy friends despise, forsake thee?*

But Scriven found the answer for all his heartaches, including the loss of friends:

> *Take it to the Lord in prayer.*
> *In His arms He'll take and shield Thee;*
> *Thou wilt find a solace there.*

The friendship of Jesus! This is a friendship without measure, without change, and without end. Our earthly friendships are not without measure. There is a limit to them. They are not without change. Sometimes they cool. They are not without end. Jesus' friendship is different. There is none like it.

Jesus says: "Greater love has no one than this, than to lay down one's life for his friends" (John 15:13).

And this is exactly what Jesus did for His people. He laid down His life on the cross for them. I sometimes think we do not fully appreciate this. We are all familiar with stories about people laying down their lives for their friends. But what Jesus did on the cross is in a completely different category. If you were to give up your life to save a friend, it would certainly be a noble act, but you would only be speeding up what is inevitable because you are already destined to die. But Jesus didn't have to die. As God, He was not subject to death. In order to die He had to take our humanity. In dying for us, He came to do what He did not have to do.

In addition to that, the kind of death Jesus died was entirely different than any other kind of death. In other words, Jesus' death was far more than a physical phenomenon. On the cross, He experienced an eternity's worth of God-forsakenness so His friends would never have to experience it.

Thank God for the friendship of Jesus! Other friendships may fail, but His never will. It begins in this life for all who come to Him in repentance and faith, and it will continue undimmed and undiminished through the ceaseless ages of eternity. If you have the friendship of Jesus, you have a Friend who will never leave your side (Heb. 13:5).

.

# -21-

# From God's Word, the Bible...

*For here we have no continuing city, but we seek the one to come.*

*Hebrews 13:14*

# No Continuing City

The author of Hebrews wrote his letter to Jews who had professed faith in the Lord Jesus Christ. All would seem to be well, but these people were in trouble. Their profession of faith had brought suffering their way. Some of their number had already been driven out of their much-loved city of Jerusalem. Others were expecting the same to happen to them.

This author wrote to encourage them. He reminded them that Jesus had been driven out of Jerusalem to Golgotha, where He died on the cross. If Jesus was willing to do that for them, they should regard being driven out of Jerusalem for His cause as a small sacrifice indeed (Heb. 13:12-13).

Having made that argument, the author proceeds to tell them that they were mistaken to attach so much significance to the city of Jerusalem. It was not "a continuing city," and neither is any other city in this world.

This brief text never fails to warm and encourage my heart. I see a threefold division in it: a *fact*, a *promise* and a *duty*. The fact is one which no one can deny, the promise is one which no one should deny, but the duty is one which many do deny.

The *fact* which no one can deny is what I've already mentioned. Here we have no continuing city. This city, or this world, doesn't last. So we are wise not to allow ourselves to get too attached to it. It doesn't last because we don't continue in it. We die (Heb. 9:27). And the city itself will finally die. The Apostle John writes: "And the world is passing away, and the lust of it; but he who does the will of God abides forever" (1 John 2:17).

This same point is brought powerfully home in Revelation 18:21-24. There this world is pictured as another city—Babylon. And her eventual ruin is driven home in the English Standard Version rendering by a phrase that appears six times in verses 21-23. It is the phrase "no more." Like a trip hammer, it sounds: No more, no more, no more… . Babylon is "no more," and her music (v. 22), arts and crafts (v. 22), industry (v. 23), light (v. 23), and the joy of human relationships (v. 23) are "no more."

If we feel as sharply as we should the temporariness of this world, we will appreciate God's *promise*. It is a promise no one should deny. It is implied in our text by the words "the one to come." The point is clear. There is a lasting city to come. The Apostle Peter says: "…we, according to His promise, look for new heavens and a new earth in which righteousness dwells" (2 Peter 3:13).

The earthly Jerusalem will not last, but God has promised a New Jerusalem that will last (Rev. 21:1-2).

That phrase "no more" that so somberly describes the end of this world is used in Revelation 21 and 22 to gloriously describe what awaits the children of God. There will be "no more" sea, death, sorrow, crying, pain or curse.

We can confidently await the coming of the New Jerusalem because God has promised it, and God cannot lie (Titus 1:2).

So our *duty*—and our privilege—is to seek that city which is to come. We seek it by repenting of our sins and by trusting in Christ and His redeeming work on the cross. We seek it by daily living with the expectation that it will come and by ordering our lives in such a way that we show that we are already citizens of that better, lasting city. Abraham and other people of faith diligently sought it (Heb. 11:10,13-16), and we should seek it as well. This is our duty, but, alas, it is one which so many deny. They do not seek the lasting city because they are so enamored and infatuated with the passing city. Their folly will at last become clear, but when it is does it will be too late.

May God help each of us to be clearheaded and clear-sighted enough to see this world for what it is and that better world God has promised and to live now for that better world.

# -22-

# From God's Word, the Bible...

*Then David put his hand in his bag and took out a stone; and he slung it and struck the Philistine in his forehead, so that the stone sank into his forehead, and he fell on his face to the earth. So David prevailed over the Philistine with a sling and a stone, and struck the Philistine and killed him. But there was no sword in the hand of David.*

*I Samuel 17:49-50*

# David Couldn't Miss, but We Can

When nine-feet tall Goliath was tauntingly challenging the soldiers of the Israelite army, they cringed and cowered. Each one was probably saying of Goliath: "He's too big to hit!" When David saw him, he might very well have said: "He's too big to miss!"

It's true. David couldn't miss when he hurled his first stone at Goliath. But it wasn't because Goliath was so big. It was rather because that stone was guided with laser-precision by the unseen hand of the sovereign God. That stone hit Goliath in the head, he fell to the ground, and David used Goliath's own sword to behead him.

While David couldn't miss, we can. We can look right over the main thing God wants this incident to convey. This story is often used to suggest ways in which we can kill the giant problems that life can bring our way.

The trend in the last several years has been to look for life-lessons in the stories of the Old Testament. We ought to be more concerned about looking for Lord-lessons. I say this because of what the Lord Jesus Himself said to His disciples (see Luke 24:27, 44).

With that principle in place, we have to say that the account of David and Goliath is intended to point us to the Lord Jesus. Where do we find Him in this account? He is the greater David who defeated a greater Goliath to achieve a greater deliverance.

Think about the greater Goliath. The Goliath of the Philistines was a formidable foe indeed—nine feet tall with armor weighing 125 pounds. He hated the Israelites and desired nothing more than to enslave and destroy them.

As great as Goliath was, he could not begin to compare to the enemy of all mankind—Satan! Yes, he is a real person, and his desire is to first enslave and finally destroy the souls of individuals. Goliath had his sword and spear. Satan's master weapon is deception. He deceives people about themselves (telling them that they aren't sinners or that sin is not serious) and about God (telling them He doesn't exist or if He does, He will not judge sin).

That brings us to the greater David. David stepped forward as the champion of his people when they were both helpless and hopeless. Spurning Saul's heavy armor, David went out to meet the giant with his shepherd's sling and five smooth stones. It would seem that there was no way for him to succeed. But succeed he did.

Jesus is our champion. As David defeated Goliath on behalf of his own people, so Christ has defeated Satan on behalf of His own people. Jesus achieved victory for us by using an even more unlikely instrument than David's sling and stones. Jesus' instrument of victory was a Roman cross! That cross defeated Satan (Col. 2:15). The only way Satan's hold on us could be broken was for sin's hold on us to be broken. And the only way sin's hold on us could be broken was for its penalty to be paid. That is what Jesus did on the cross. He paid the penalty for sin so all who believe in Him will not have to pay it themselves.

The author of Hebrews calls his readers to rejoice that "through death" the Lord Jesus destroys him "who had the power of death, that is, the devil" and He, Jesus, releases those who were "subject to bondage" (Heb. 2:14-15).

What Jesus did on the cross achieves a far greater deliverance than David achieved for the Israelites. Their deliverance was temporal and temporary. It was still possible for another enemy to arise to defeat and enslave them. The deliverance provided by Jesus is eternal. Those who trust in Him can never be enslaved by Satan again. All who believe in the Lord Jesus are delivered from slavery to Satan in this life and in the life to come.

Is it okay to look for life-lessons in the story of David and Goliath? Yes, but we should always treat such lessons as secondary. The primary thing is the work of Jesus. Let's be sure not to miss that!

# -23-

# From God's Word, the Bible...

*"According to their uncleanness and according to their transgressions I have dealt with them, and hidden My face from them."*

*"And I will not hide My face from them anymore; for I shall have poured out My Spirit on the house of Israel," says the Lord GOD.*

*From Ezekiel 39:21-29*

# God's Face Hidden and Unhidden

It's not something we like to think about, but it is a reality. I'm talking about God hiding His face from His people.

We have one example of it in the passage before us. Ezekiel had been called by God to prophesy to the people of God who were in captivity in Babylon.

Why did God send His people into captivity? He tells us very plainly: "…the house of Israel went into captivity for their iniquity; because they were unfaithful to Me, therefore I hid My face from them" (v. 23).

God also says: "According to their uncleanness and according to their transgressions I have dealt with them, and hidden My face from them" (v. 24).

In sending His people into captivity, God was simply carrying out the very thing He said He would do if His people forsook Him and broke His covenant: "Then My anger shall be aroused against them in that day, and I will forsake them, and I will hide My face from them" (Deut. 31:17).

God proceeds to say: "And I will surely hide My face in that day because of all the evil which they have done, in that they have turned to other gods" (Deut. 31:18).

What are the sins of today's church that are causing God to hide His face from her? Is it refusing to preach the truth and sin and judgment to come in order to build a religious empire? Is it pride? Is it idolatry? Is it dissension and rivalry?

And what about us as individuals? What are our sins? What are we doing to hide God's face? What are we failing to do?

God doesn't hide His face from His people to be cruel and mean to them. He does it to correct them. In Ezekiel 39 we find the Lord anticipating that day when His correction of His people would be complete. Here is what He says: "… I will not hide My face from them anymore; for I shall have poured out My Spirit on the house of Israel…" (v. 39).

It is vital that we make this connection—the opposite of God hiding His face is Him pouring out His Spirit.

To say God is hiding His face is to say that He is not pouring out His Spirit. And to say God is not pouring out His Spirit is to say that nothing of any value can be accomplished in our churches as long as the Spirit is withheld.

What are God's people to do when He is hiding His face from them? What must we do if are to enjoy once again the unhidden face of God? Here is another way to put it: If God is hiding His face from His people, what does He expect them to do?

The answer, I suggest, is supplied in these words that David spoke to God:

> *When You said, "Seek My face,"*
> *My heart said to You,*
> *"Your face, LORD, I will seek."*
> (Ps. 27:8)

The answer is plain to see. If God is hiding His face from us, He wants us to seek His face. If our sins cause Him to hide His face, then to seek His face means we must turn from our sins in true repentance. Are we doing this? Are we seeking God's face through heartfelt repentance, or are we content to go along as we are?

Although Christians frequently fail, they never have to be concerned about losing their salvation. In other words, they never have to be concerned about God hiding His face from them in eternity (Rev. 22:3-5). And what's the reason God's people don't have to fear Him hiding His face from them in eternity? It's because He hid His face from Jesus when He, Jesus, was on the cross. If God hides His face from sin and Jesus became sin for us (2 Cor. 5:21), God had to hide His face from Jesus. If we turn from our sins and trust in the Lord Jesus, it will be our enormous privilege to "see His face" throughout eternity (Rev. 22:4).

# -24-

# From God's Word, the Bible...

*Let the word of Christ dwell in you richly in all wisdom, teaching and admonishing one another in psalms and hymns and spiritual songs, singing with grace in your hearts to the Lord.*

*Colossians 3:16*

# A Rich Dwelling

In this text the Apostle Paul urges his readers to let the Word of Christ dwell "richly" within them.

We find the word of Christ in the Bible. The Bible consists of many, many words, but it is essentially one word. It has one message, and that is the message of Christ. It is the Word of God, and since Christ is God, it is also the Word of Christ. The Bible is Christ speaking about Christ!

In the Bible the Lord Jesus Christ tells us that God, our Creator, is holy and righteous, and He demands that we have perfect righteousness or He will not admit us into heaven (Rev. 21:27). The Lord Jesus also tells us that we do not have the righteousness that God requires. Each of us has broken God's laws time after time. God demands righteousness, and we don't have it. Thankfully, the Lord Jesus tells us about Himself. He tells us that He does have the righteousness God demands, and His righteousness can be counted as ours if we will trust Him as our Lord and Savior. What about all our sins? The Lord Jesus tells us in the Bible that His death on the cross paid the penalty for those who believe. Here is Christianity in a nutshell—Jesus got our sins, and we get His righteousness.

It should be obvious to us that we have in the Bible an immeasurable treasure. It's no wonder David said to the Lord:

> *I have rejoiced in the way of Your testimonies,*
> *As much as in all riches.*
> (Ps. 119:14)

> *The law of Your mouth is better to me*
> *Than thousands of shekels of gold and silver.*
> (Ps. 119:72)

> *I rejoice at Your word*
> *As one who finds great treasure.*
> (Ps. 119:162)

The question is not whether we have enormous riches in the Bible. It is rather whether we are letting those riches dwell richly in us. It is not enough, however, to hold the Bible in our hands. We must hold it in our hearts, treasuring it for its richness.

So how do we let the Word of Christ dwell richly within? It's obvious that we must read it, but we must ever be on guard against the tendency to merely read words. How easy it is for us to do our daily Bible reading only to come away without being able to tell anyone what we read. To read the Bible well, we have to read it:

- confidently, knowing it is true and dependable (Ps. 119:142,151,160; 2 Tim. 3:16; 2 Peter 1:21)
- joyfully (Ps. 119:14,162; Jer. 15:16)
- diligently (Acts 17:11; 2 Tim. 2:15)
- reverently (Ps. 119:161; Isa. 66:2,5)

- Christocentrically, that is, looking for the Lord Jesus who is its subject and focus (Luke 24:27,44-45; John 5:39; Acts 8:35; 2 Tim. 3:14-15)
- experientially (Is there a promise for me to believe? A command for me to obey? An example for me to copy?)

Furthermore, if we are to have the Bible dwelling richly within us, we must give priority to regularly attending public worship services in which the message of the Bible is faithfully preached and taught. But it's not enough to merely park our bodies on church pews. We must discipline ourselves to listen—really listen—to the preaching and teaching of God's Word, saying to the Lord: "Speak, for Your servant hears" (1 Sam. 3:10).

Those of us who have been blessed to be part of God-honoring, Christ-exalting, Bible-preaching churches for years should constantly remind ourselves that our blessing can become our curse. Familiarity with the Scriptures is a blessing, but when we allow that familiarity to cause us not to eagerly listen, it is a curse. We should come to each event of the preaching and teaching of the Word as if we were hearing it for the first time.

I want to be rich, but I hope I know what it is to be rich. It is not a matter of what I dwell in but rather what dwells in me, and to what degree it dwells there.

Lord, may Your Word dwell richly in me.

# -25-

## From God's Word, the Bible...

*Beloved, I beg you as sojourners and pilgrims, abstain from fleshly lusts which war against the soul, having your conduct honorable among the Gentiles, that when they speak against you as evildoers, they may, by your good works which they observe, glorify God in the day of visitation.*

*1 Peter 2:11-12*
*(Read 1 Peter 3:8-17 and 1 Peter 4:12-19 for this meditation, too)*

# What About Christophobia?

Lots of "phobias" are being tossed around these days—Islamaphobia, homophobia, xenophobia, to mention just a few such terms.

Express a viewpoint that is out of keeping with the political correctness of our day, and you will likely find yourself labeled as a "phobe" of one kind or another, and as far as the labelers are concerned, nothing could possibly be worse. And, of course, those who are so eager to apply the "phobe" tag to others congratulate themselves on being free from such phobias. But are they?

The same people who warn us about various phobias are ever vigilant to warn us about hatred and hate crimes.

There is one phobia that appears to be growing by leaps and bounds, but it is never mentioned. It is Christophobia, that is, fear of Christianity or fear of Christians. Those who enjoy tossing the phobia label around have no interest in Christophobia. Could it be that they are Christophobes?

And many of those who lecture us about hatred don't hesitate to express their hatred for Christians and Christianity. Is there a double standard at work here?

Hatred toward any individual or group is obviously wrong, and Christians oppose it. But we have reached the point where no one can disagree with any aspect of the political correctness of our day without being tagged as a hater. Disagreement is now hatred!

Interestingly enough, many who hate Christianity openly admit it. But they argue that their hatred is justified. Associating Christianity with oppression of African-Americans, women, and homosexuals, they believe that they can't champion the rights of those groups without hating Christianity. Have Christians been guilty of such oppressions? It is more correct to say that *professing* Christians have been guilty of many heinous things, but one of the fundamental teachings of the Bible is that not all who profess to be Christians are, in fact, what they profess. The haters of Christianity never make that distinction. Their hatred for the Christian faith is such that they will seize the wrong thinking and wrongdoing of a professing Christians and attribute the same to all Christians. They tar all with the same brush.

This isn't to say that even true Christians are perfect in all their views and acts. They aren't. But as believers in Christ grow in their understanding of His teachings, they come to see their errors and endeavor to correct them.

Many of the Christophobes of our day are simply misinformed. They associate Christianity with oppression, but they have never bothered to thoroughly research what Christians have done to fight oppression, relieve suffering, and attain equality. They don't delve into such matters because that would destroy their narrative, and they are very eager to maintain that narrative.

How are Christians to respond to the increasing number

of Christophobes in our day? We need to be very careful to live in a like Christlike manner. We need to seek to disarm and discredit our critics by engaging in such good conduct that they will find it hard to apply their labels and express their hatred.

And in the hatred of Christianity, we can and should find reason to be grateful. Grateful? Yes! It is a delicious irony that those who hate Christianity show by that very hatred that Christianity is true. Jesus clearly predicted that His followers would be hated (John 15:18-25), and every hateful word and deed that comes our way proves those words to be true.

An old story has soldiers shooting their arrows skyward because they were angry with the gods, only to have those arrows fall on their own heads. So the hatred of Christianity has a way of coming back on those who nurse such views.

Finally, we must also respond to the hatred of Christians by looking forward to that day when the Lord Jesus Christ and those who know Him will be fully vindicated. These are days in which we should cling tenaciously to these words: "These will make war with the Lamb, and the Lamb will overcome them, for He is Lord of lords and King of kings; and those who are with Him are called, chosen, and faithful" (Rev. 17:14).

While we wait for that day of victory, let's be thankful we can suffer in some measure for the Christ who suffered so much to make the victory a reality.

# -26-

# From God's Word, the Bible...

*Praise the LORD!*
*For it is good to sing praises to our God;*
*For it is pleasant, and praise is beautiful.*
*The LORD builds up Jerusalem;*
*He gathers together the outcasts of Israel.*
*He heals the brokenhearted*
*And binds up their wounds.*
*He counts the number of the stars;*
*He calls them all by name.*
*Great is our Lord, and mighty in power;*
*His understanding is infinite.*
*The LORD lifts up the humble;*
*He casts the wicked down to the ground.*

*Psalm 147:1-6*

# Broken Hearts, Numbered Stars

The old preacher J.C. Ryle used to say: "Heart-trouble is the commonest thing in the world."[3] He was not talking about the heart as a physical organ. He was talking about sorrow of heart or brokenheartedness.

The original readers of Psalm 147 knew about the broken heart. They were in captivity in Babylon. Their city, the city of Jerusalem, was in ruins. The beautiful temple built by Solomon was a pile of rubble. Homes were gone. Family members were separated.

The question that frequently echoed in their heads was this: "Does God care?"

This psalmist wrote to give them the answer. He assured them that God would gather them, that is, bring them home, and in doing so would heal their broken hearts.

---

[3] *Expository Thoughts on John*, vol. 3, Edinburgh, The Banner of Truth Trust, p.55

This author sets forth an unusual treatment for broken hearts. We can call it the therapy of the stars. Have you noticed it? Immediately after telling them that God heals the brokenhearted, he says God numbers the stars. How does he get from the former to the latter?

Think about the stars. If we could take a ride on a beam of light, we would be traveling 186,000 miles per second. That means we would go around the earth seven times each second. If we could ride our beam for 6,000 years, we would be only one-tenth of the way across our galaxy, and, there are billions of galaxies.

All of this led the psalmist to say:

> *Great is our Lord, and mighty in power;*
> *His understanding is infinite.*
> (Ps. 147:5)

The point is that our God is more than sufficient for healing our broken hearts.

Someone might say: "That doesn't help at all. It only makes me feel like an insignificant speck. It makes me feel as if God doesn't know about my broken heart."

But we are not through with the therapy of the stars. The psalmist assures us that God knows the stars individually— "He calls them all by name" (v. 4). Countless numbers of stars—gazillions of them—and God knows each one and has named each of them.

If God knows each star by name, why should we doubt that he knows all about us?

The therapy of the stars is great—God is sufficient for us and God has individual knowledge of us. But it must finally give way to the therapy of the cross. Christians should not doubt that God knows and cares for His brokenhearted people because of the cross. He put His Son there to provide healing for the worst problem of all—the guilt of our sins. If God has already demonstrated on the cross His care for the greatest of our problems, how can we doubt that He cares about all our lesser problems?

Then there is that nasty question that is always hanging on the edge of any discussion about God's people having broken hearts. If God is as great as this psalmist says, He could obviously prevent His people from ever being brokenhearted. So why does God allow our hearts to be broken?

I'm sure that Joseph wondered why God allowed him to experience the brokenheartedness of being hated by his brothers, sold into slavery, and falsely accused and imprisoned. But while it didn't make sense to him at the time, he was able to say to his brothers at the end: "But as for you, you meant evil against me; but God meant it for good..." (Gen. 50:20)

We may not get to see God's purpose come full circle in this life as Joseph did. We may live out our lives with our whys. Let's always remember that final healing for broken hearts takes place in heaven. There we will learn why God worked in our lives as He did, and there it will all make perfect sense.

> *Trials dark on every hand,*
> *And we cannot understand,*
> *All the ways that God would lead us*
> *To that blessed promised land;*
> *But He'll guide us with His eye,*
> *And we'll follow till we die;*
> *We will understand it better by and by.*
> (Charles A. Tindley)

… # -27-

# From God's Word, the Bible...

*…for the Son of Man has come to seek and to save that which was lost.*

*Luke 19:10*

# Is Christianity Boring?

Lots of people, especially young people, refuse to attend church services because they find such services to be boring. So, the thinking goes, it's up to church leaders to get "boring" out of church. The best way to do so? The answer seems to be to replace it, "boring," with "entertaining."

In the effort to swap the one for the other, all kinds of things are being done. One pastor even preached in his pajamas! Are we really to believe that the sight of a pastor in pajamas caused many in the congregation to say: "Oh, good, the preacher is in his pajamas! Now I'm not bored!"

We have reached the point where all kinds of outlandish behavior is being condoned in churches in the interest of fighting boredom and making Christianity relevant and interesting.

Think about it! Christianity as it is presented in the Bible—and there is no other kind—isn't interesting. It's boring, and it's up to us to rescue it.

The syllogism driving many church leaders these days is as follows:

- Christianity is boring.
- People don't want to be bored.
- Christianity must be changed.

But this is a sorry syllogism. It doesn't even get off the ground. Its first premise is faulty. Christianity isn't boring. Those who find it to be so only reveal that they don't understand it.

What is Christianity? It is God's rescue mission. It is God rescuing sinners from the peril awaiting them.

Rescue from peril is not boring. When a fireman bursts into fire and smoke to rescue a woman, she doesn't say, "That was certainly boring." When a lifeguard saves a man from drowning, he doesn't say, "That was terribly boring."

We aren't bored when our personal survival or wellbeing is at stake. If you had handed me a paper dealing with skull fractures several years ago, I would have said: "I find this to be very boring." But then I suffered a skull fracture, and, guess what, I got very interested in skull fractures. What changed? My wellbeing wouldn't have been at stake at the time you handed me the paper, but it was when I had the skull fracture.

The fire, the rolling waves, and the skull fracture are serious perils, but they can't begin to compare to the one facing the sinner. That is the greatest peril of all. It is the peril of "flaming fire" in "everlasting destruction" (2 Thess. 1:8,9). It is the peril of weeping and gnashing of teeth (Matt. 13:42,50). It is the peril of the darkest darkness imaginable (Jude 13).

Do our sins really merit such things? Consider this: all sin is directed against the infinite God, and we have all sinned time after time without regard to God's warnings.

What is appropriate punishment for numberless sins against an infinite person who has warned us again and again?

Some are ever eager to diminish the Bible's teachings on eternal peril by suggesting that the fire, the darkness, and the wailing constitute figurative language. But what kind of reality is it that requires such language to describe it? It must be a horrible reality indeed.

The good news is that the God against whom we have sinned rescues sinners from their peril. He sent His Son, the Lord Jesus Christ, to this earth in our humanity. Jesus came on a rescue mission. On the cross He paid the penalty that sinners deserve so they don't have to pay that same penalty. He endured the wrath of God in the place of all who will trust in Him. People who describe Christianity as boring only reveal that they have never understood God or what Jesus did on the cross. That assessment of the Christian faith tells us a lot more about them than it tells us about Christianity.

Christianity is God loving people who have spat in His face and offended Him again and again despite all the goodness He has shown to them. Let me personalize it. It is God Himself rescuing me from hell by taking my hell in the person of His Son. Because of what God has done, I no longer have to fear condemnation but wait with eager anticipation the glory of heaven. If that is boring, please count me among the bored.

# -28-

# From God's Word, the Bible...

*But God, who is rich in mercy, because of His great love with which He loved us, even when we were dead in trespasses, made us alive together with Christ (by grace you have been saved), and raised us up together, and made us sit together in the heavenly places in Christ Jesus, that in the ages to come He might show the exceeding riches of His grace in His kindness toward us in Christ Jesus.*

*Ephesians 2:4-7*

# My Favorite Words

It is not unusual to hear people speak about a favorite color, a favorite place, a favorite song or a favorite food. We may even hear someone refer to a favorite uncle, aunt or cousin. We almost never hear anyone talk about a favorite word or words.

I can't say I have a favorite color, place, food or relative, but I do have favorite words.

At the top of the list is the word *grace*. As far as I'm concerned, it is the queen of words. I'm not referring to the word as it is often used. If someone exhibits unusual elegance or poise, that person may be described as having "grace." While I certainly do not object to the word being used in that way, it is not what I have in mind. I'm referring rather to the grace of God in the matter of salvation for sinners.

What is grace? It is God freely bestowing on sinners everything they need to be forgiven of their sins and to be in a right standing with Him. It is God refusing to give to sinners what they deserve and giving them what they don't deserve.

Grace is God doing the following:

- setting His heart on sinners even before the world began;
- providing in Christ the righteousness sinners don't have and payment for the sins they do have;
- working in their minds and hearts so they can receive Christ in what He has done;
- causing them to grow and mature so they conform more and more to the image of Christ;
- preserving them in their faith;
- bringing them safely home to glory.

Some think of salvation in terms of God doing His part and us doing our part; but grace emphasizes that there is only one part to salvation, and it is God's.

*Propitiation* is another of my favorite words. It takes us to the very heart of what the Lord Jesus did on the cross. There He propitiated, that is He satisfied or appeased, the wrath of God.

I often find myself thinking that the main thing people don't know about God is that He is holy. Or perhaps they don't understand what that means. Yes, it means God is free from all moral failure or blemish, but it also means He can't simply ignore sin. The Bible speaks of God's deep aversion to sin. It speaks of God "burning" in anger against it and "vomiting" at the sight of it.

God has real wrath against sinners. Before He can enter into a relationship with them, that wrath has to be satisfied. Jesus went to the cross for the express purpose of satisfying that wrath. The wrath of God fell on Jesus there on the cross, and there is no wrath now for those who repent of their sins and trust in the Lord Jesus Christ. Keith Getty puts it in these words:

*This, the pow'r of the cross:*
*Christ became sin for us;*
*Took the blame, bore the wrath –*
*We stand forgiven at the cross.*

*This, the pow'r of the cross:*
*Son of God—slain for us.*
*What a love! What a cost!*
*We stand forgiven at the cross.*

I have yet another word to add to the list of my favorite words. It is *mediator*. A mediator is one who steps between parties in conflict and makes peace. Jesus is our mediator, and He is the only possible mediator (1 Tim. 2:5). He is the God-man, fully God and fully man at one and the same time. So in the conflict between God and man, He can fully represent both. As God, He provided the redemption we need. As man, He received what our sins deserve.

Grace! Propitiation! Mediator! What marvelous words! Because of them we can have salvation. I love those words, but, come to think of it, there may be one word I love more—*saved*!

*I've found a Friend, who is all to me,*
*His love is ever true;*
*I love to tell how He lifted me*
*And what His grace can do for you.*
*Saved by His pow'r divine,*
*Saved to new life sublime!*
*Life now is sweet and my joy is complete,*
*For I'm saved, saved, saved!*
(Jack P. Scholfield)

# -29-

# From God's Word, the Bible...

*For I determined not to know anything among you except Jesus Christ and Him crucified.*

*1 Corinthians 2:2*

*But God forbid that I should boast except in the cross of our Lord Jesus Christ, by whom the world has been crucified to me, and I to the world.*

*Galatians 6:14*

# That Great Thing

If you were asked to name the one great thing in your life, what would you say? What is that one thing that dominates and dwarfs all other things? What is the thing that you live for?

Many would not hesitate to name their family or their health or their financial wellbeing as their one great thing. Less discerning people might name sports or sexual pleasure or dining on fine food.

In his hymn *Ask Ye What Great Thing I Know*, Johann C. Schwedler (1672-1730) invites us to ask him to name his great thing. "Go ahead and ask me," he says. "Yes," he says, "ask me to name the thing that 'delights and stirs me so.'"

Have you ever seen a child so eager to answer a question that he or she begs the teacher to call on him or her?

Schwedler is like that child. He wants us to ask because he is ever so eager to give us his answer. He's afraid that we won't ask, but one gets the impression from his hymn that he would tell us even if we didn't ask.

So we give in to his eagerness. "Okay, Schwedler, we'll

bite. Anything to get you to stop waving your arms at us and jumping up and down! What is your great thing?"

And Schwedler, relieved that we have finally asked, says—are you ready for this?—"Jesus Christ, the crucified."

This is Schwedler's great thing? A Jewish carpenter turned rabbi hanging on a Roman cross about 2,000 years ago? That's the great thing? Schwedler must have been out of his mind!

Was Schwedler crazy, or is it possible that he saw something in the cross of Jesus that most have never seen, something of such amazing significance that if they were to see it, they would join Schwedler in naming it as their great thing? And what did Schwedler see? He tells us that the cross was the place where Jesus "bore my sinful load" and "purchased for me peace with God."

You will never join Schwedler in his assessment of the cross if you never come to see your "sinful load." Sin is the greatest load in the world. What is sin? It is refusing to live the way God, our Creator and Ruler, wants us to live. It is thumbing our noses in His face and saying: "We don't care about how You want us to live. We will live the way we want to live."

God tells us that we must be one hundred per cent righteous before He will allow us to enter into heaven. Can you imagine meeting this God who demands that we be perfectly righteous? Can you imagine standing before him loaded down with your sin and guilt?

The fact is that our sins must be forgiven before we can ever enter the presence of God for eternity, and God cannot forgive our sins until the penalty He has pronounced on our sins is carried out. For God to forgive our sins without honoring that penalty would amount to His denying His own justice and compromising His character.

That brings us to the cross. It was there that Jesus took

the penalty for sinners. He actually bore the "sinful load" there. The wrath of God against our sins was poured out on Him so that all who repent of their sins and believe in Him will never have to bear that penalty themselves.

Sin puts us at odds with God. But when sin is forgiven through Christ's atoning death, we have peace with God.

If you look at Jesus' death on the cross as just another man dying another death, Schwedler's hymn will sound absurd. But if you understand your "sinful load" and what Jesus did about it, you will gladly join him in singing:

> *What is faith's foundation strong?*
> *What awakes my heart to song?*
> *He who bore my sinful load,*
> *Purchased for me peace with God,*
> *Jesus Christ, the crucified.*
> *This is the great thing I know:*
> *This delights and stirs me so:*
> *Faith in him who died to save,*
> *Him who triumphed o'er the grave:*
> *Jesus Christ, the crucified.*

# -30-

# From God's Word, the Bible...

*I waited patiently for the LORD;*
*And He inclined to me,*
*And heard my cry.*
*He also brought me up out of a horrible pit,*
*Out of the miry clay,*
*And set my feet upon a rock,*
*And established my steps.*
*He has put a new song in my mouth—*
*Praise to our God;*
*Many will see it and fear,*
*And will trust in the LORD.*

*Psalm 40:1-3*

# God's Glad Man

His name was Billy Bray. He was born in 1794 in a tin-mining community in southwestern England.

In his younger years, Billy lived, as he put it, "very near hell." He was such a drunkard that each night his wife would go to the tavern to help him home. He was such a blasphemer that his friends said his words came from hell itself because they smelled of sulfur.

But Billy Bray was converted to Christ in November of 1823, and praise to God became the dominant feature of his life. He would often say: "If they were to put me in a barrel, I would shout glory out through the plug-hole!"

Some of his friends scoffed at his conversion and suggested that he had gone mad. Here's how Billy responded: "They said I was a mad-man, but they meant I was a glad-man, and, glory be to God! I have been glad ever since."

Nearing his seventy-fourth birthday and feeling very ill, Billy went to a doctor. "You are going to die," the doctor somberly said. Upon receiving such news, many would sit in stunned silence. Others would break down and sob. Not

Billy! He shouted: "Glory! Glory be to God! I shall soon be in heaven!"

Then Billy turned to the doctor and asked: "When I get up there, shall I tell them that you will be coming too?"

As wonderful and compelling as the story of Billy Bray is, it contains elements of danger. We must not be led astray by Billy Bray! One danger is to think that we must be as bad as he was before we need to be saved. This is the conclusion many draw. They think Christianity is only for those who have plumbed the depths of wickedness. The truth is we are all sinners, and, as such, we all need to be saved (Rom. 3:10,23). To put it another way, we all come into this world in a state of spiritual deadness. We are alive to sin but dead to God. Among dead people, there are degrees of decay, but there are no degrees of deadness. Dead is dead! The person who died a hundred years ago is more decayed than the one who died five minutes ago, but they are both dead. Some sinners are more decayed than others, but all are equally dead, and need, therefore, spiritual life from God.

The message of Christianity is clear—no one is too bad to be saved, and no one is too good to be saved!

Another danger is to think that we must be exactly like Billy Bray after we are saved. Conversion to Christ doesn't obliterate our personalities. Those who are quiet and reserved before they are saved will manifest those qualities after they are saved. And those who, like Billy, are exuberant by nature will show that same exuberance after they are saved.

But while Christians have differing personalities, they have this in common—the element of praise. While each will express that praise in keeping with his or her personality type, it will be present. Every Christian can say of the Lord:

> *He has made me glad, He has made me glad,*
> *I will rejoice for he has made me glad.*
> *He has made me glad, He has made me glad,*
> *I will rejoice for he has made me glad.*

The other side of the coin is this: we shouldn't be too quick to use our personality types to excuse ourselves from more exuberant praise. It could be that Billy's life of praise was not so much a product of his personality as it was of his understanding. In other words, he might very well have praised God more exuberantly for salvation than others because he understood salvation more than they. The explanation for Billy Bray may be that he let the words of Isaiah 12:1-2 sink more deeply into his mind and heart than most of us ever will:

> *O LORD, I will praise You;*
> *Though You were angry with me,*
> *Your anger is turned away, and You comfort me.*
> *Behold, God is my salvation,*
> *I will trust and not be afraid;*
> *"For YAH, the LORD, is my strength and my song;*
> *He also has become my salvation."*

# -31-

# From God's Word, the Bible...

*The lot is cast into the lap,*
*But its every decision is from the LORD.*
*Proverbs 16:33*

*The king's heart is in the hand of the LORD,*
*Like the rivers of water;*
*He turns it wherever He wishes.*
*Proverbs 21:1*

*The horse is prepared for the day of battle,*
*But deliverance is of the LORD.*
*Proverbs 21:31*

# The Shot That Was Never Fired

A Union soldier had guard duty one night. He watched and watched, but he didn't see. What was it that he didn't see? A Confederate soldier pointing his rifle at him! The trigger was never pulled. The shot was never fired. The Union soldier was spared. And the name of the spared soldier? It was none other than Ira D. Sankey. Sankey, the famous gospel singer? Yes, one and the same.

What was it that caused the Confederate soldier not to fire the deadly shot? Amazingly enough, Sankey began singing a hymn just as the soldier was about to squeeze the trigger, and the hymn was none other than the Confederate's favorite. So he listened a while, stole away in the night, and Sankey lived.

It's not enough to merely say Sankey lived. How he lived! He went on to be associated with D. L. Moody. He sang in Moody's crusades, and in so doing brought blessing to multitudes of people.

Sankey never knew how close he came to death that night until years later. It was Christmas Eve of 1876, and Sankey was on board a boat on the Delaware River. Someone recognized him, and immediately several crowded around to ask if he would sing a Christmas hymn. For some reason Sankey chose not to sing a Christmas song but rather *Savior, Like a Shepherd Lead Us*.

When Sankey finished singing, a man approached to ask a series of questions. Had he, Sankey, served in the Union army? Yes. Did he remember having guard duty at a particular place in 1862? Yes. Did he remember singing that very song while on guard duty? Yes. It was then that Sankey learned about the shot that was not fired.

It would certainly have been a great loss if Sankey had been killed on the night that he was posted to watch. So what about that shot that was never fired? How are we to explain it? Was it only a remarkable coincidence that Sankey began to sing at the precise moment that his life was hanging in the balance? Was it another remarkable coincidence that he chose to sing the Confederate soldier's favorite hymn? Many would say so. But Christians do not believe in coincidence. They believe in providence.

Providence is God managing and controlling even the smallest circumstances to the glory of His name and the good of His people.

The sparing of Sankey's life was certainly a kind providence. It's obvious to us that God had important work for Sankey to do. But there are also those providences which Christians call "strange" or "hard." These are providences that don't make sense to us. They are those in which God sends difficulties into the lives of His people. Great faith dares to believe that even God's hard providences are kind, that even in them God has our best interests at heart and is working for our good.

At the time, it may have seemed a hard providence for Paul to have his path blocked while he was seeking to advance God's kingdom. Having to be in Troas was not what he wanted. There were many other difficult circumstances he faced—shipwrecks, beatings, persecutions to name just a few! His words in Acts 14:22 still apply today: "We must through many tribulations enter the kingdom of God." In it all, he knew from the words God gave him, Romans 8:28, that "…all things work together for good to those who love God, to those who are the called according to His purpose."

The hard providences of life should cause us to love the words of Charles A. Tindley:

*Trials dark on every hand,*
*And we cannot understand*
*All the ways that God would lead us*
*To that blessed promised land;*
*But He'll guide us with His eye,*
*And we'll follow till we die;*
*We will understand it better by and by.*

One of the most exquisite delights of heaven will be learning about the hard providences that came our way, and another will be learning about the same in the lives others.

The supreme example of a hard providence is the one that God Himself endured. It was a hard providence that caused men to despise Jesus and nail Him to a cruel cross. But through that hard providence, God has provided salvation for all sinners who will turn away from sin and trust in Christ. Until we learn in heaven all the meanings of all God's providences, let us sing:

*Savior, like a shepherd lead us,*
*Much we need Thy tender care…*

# About the Author

Roger Ellsworth is a retired pastor, active in ministry and writing, who lives in Jackson, Tennessee. He and his wife, Sylvia, love the message of the Bible, and they enjoy sharing the wonderful counsel of the Word of God in language that ordinary people can understand and appreciate.

Roger has written numerous books on the Christian faith, and has exercised a preaching ministry for over fifty years. His sermons are available to listen for free on SermonAudio.com.

# Other Books

*Enjoy collecting the My Coffee Cup Meditations Series.*

*The "Thumbs-Up" Man ISBN 978-0-9988812-5-6*
*A Dog and A Clock ISBN 978-0-9988812-9-4*
*When God Blocks Our Path ISBN 978-0-9988812-4-9*

www.mycoffeecupmeditations.com

www.ingramcontent.com/pod-product-compliance
Lightning Source LLC
Chambersburg PA
CBHW070623300426
44113CB00010B/1640